MW01005171

Leveled Texts
for Social Studies

The 20th Century

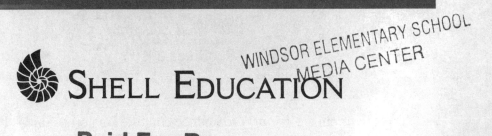

WINDSOR ELEMENTARY SCHOOL
MEDIA CENTER

SHELL EDUCATION

Paid For By
Lottery Money

Reading Level Consultant
Debra J. Housel, M.S.Ed.

English Language Learner Consultants
D. Kyle Shuler
Chino Valley Unified School District, California
Marcela von Vacano
Arlington County Schools, Virginia

Gifted Education Consultant/Editor
Wendy Conklin, M.A.

Special Education Consultant
Dennis Benjamin

Contributing Content Authors
Debra J. Housel, M.S.Ed.
Lisa Zamosky
Wendy Conklin, M.A.
Christine Dugan, M.A.Ed.
Blane Conklin, Ph.D.

Publisher
Corinne Burton, M.A.Ed.

Associate Editor
Torrey Maloof

Editorial Assistant
Kathryn R. Kiley

Editorial Director
Emily R. Smith, M.A.Ed.

Editor-in-Chief
Sharon Coan, M.S.Ed.

Editorial Manager
Gisela Lee, M.A.

Creative Director
Lee Aucoin

Designer
Neri Garcia

Cover Art
Library of Congress

Shell Education

5301 Oceanus Drive

Huntington Beach, CA 92649

http://www.shelleducation.com

ISBN 978-1-4258-0084-0

© 2008 Shell Education

Reprinted 2010

The classroom teacher may reproduce copies of materials in this book for classroom use only. The reproduction of any part for an entire school or school system is strictly prohibited. No part of this publication may be transmitted, stored, or recorded in any form without written permission from the publisher.

Table of Contents

Introduction

   What Is Differentiation? 4

   How to Differentiate Using This Product...5

   General Information About the Student Populations...............................6–8

      Special Education Students...6

      English Language Learners..6

      Regular Education Students..7

      Gifted Education Students 8

   Strategies for Using the Leveled Texts..9–17

      Special Education Students...9

      English Language Learners...13

      Gifted Education Students 16

   How to Use This Product 18–20

      Readability Chart..18

      Components of the Product..19

      Tips for Managing the Product...20

Leveled Texts

   The Industrial Revolution 21–28

   Men of the Industrial Revolution...29–36

   European Immigration 37–44

   Asian Immigration 45–52

   World War I: The "Great War" 53–60

   The Roaring Twenties..61–68

   The Great Depression 69–76

   World War II in Europe..77–84

   World War II in the Pacific..85–92

   World War II Leaders 93–100

   The Civil Rights Movement 101–108

   Dr. Martin Luther King Jr. 109–116

   The Cold War...117–124

   Conflicts in the Middle East..125–132

   Modern World Leaders 133–140

Appendix

   Resources..141

      References Cited...141

      Image Sources..141–143

      Contents of Teacher Resource CD...144

What Is Differentiation?

Over the past few years, classrooms have evolved into diverse pools of learners. Gifted students, English language learners, learning-disabled students, high achievers, underachievers, and average students all come together to learn from one teacher. The teacher is expected to meet their diverse needs in one classroom. It brings back memories of the one-room schoolhouse during early American history. Not too long ago, lessons were designed to be one size fits all. It was thought that students in the same grade level learned in similar ways. Today, we know that viewpoint to be faulty. Students have differing learning styles, come from different cultures, experience a variety of emotions, and have varied interests. For each subject, they also differ in academic readiness. At times, the challenges teachers face can be overwhelming as they struggle to figure out how to create learning environments that address the differences they find in their students.

What is differentiation? Carol Ann Tomlinson at the University of Virginia says, "Differentiation is simply a teacher attending to the learning needs of a particular student or small group of students, rather than teaching a class as though all individuals in it were basically alike" (2000). Differentiation can be carried out by any teacher who keeps the learners at the forefront of his or her instruction. The effective teacher asks, "What am I going to do to shape instruction to meet the needs of all my learners?" One method or methodology will not reach all students.

Differentiation encompasses what is taught, how it is taught, and the products students create to show what they have learned. When differentiating curriculum, teachers become the organizers of learning opportunities within the classroom environment. These categories are often referred to as content, process, and product.

- **Content:** Differentiating the content means to put more depth into the curriculum through organizing the curriculum concepts and structure of knowledge.
- **Process:** Differentiating the process requires the use of varied instructional techniques and materials to enhance the learning of students.
- **Product:** When products are differentiated, cognitive development and the students' abilities to express themselves improve.

Teachers should differentiate content, process, and product according to students' characteristics. These characteristics include students' readiness, learning styles, and interests.

- **Readiness:** If learning experiences align closely with students' previous skills and understanding of topics, they will learn better.
- **Learning styles:** Teachers should create assignments that allow students to complete work according to their personal preferences and styles.
- **Interests:** If a topic sparks excitement in the learners, then students will become involved in learning and better remember what is taught.

How to Differentiate Using This Product

The leveled texts in this series help teachers differentiate social studies content for their students. Each book has 15 topics, and each topic has a text written at four different reading levels. (See page 19 for more information.) These texts are written at a variety of reading levels, but all the levels remain strong in presenting the social studies content and vocabulary. Teachers can focus on the same content standard or objective for the whole class, but individual students can access the content at their *instructional* levels rather than at their *frustration* levels.

Determining your students' instructional reading levels is the first step in the process. It is important to assess their reading abilities often so they do not get tracked into one level. Below are suggested ways to use this resource as well as other resources to determine students' reading levels.

- **Running records:** While your class is doing independent work, pull your below-grade-level students aside, one at a time. Individually have them read aloud the lowest level of a text (the star level) as you record any errors they make on your own copy of the text. If students read accurately and fluently and comprehend the material, move them up to the next level and repeat the process. Following the reading, ask comprehension questions to assess their understanding of the material. Assess their accuracy and fluency, mark the words they say incorrectly, and listen for fluent reading. Use your judgment to determine whether students seem frustrated as they read. As a general guideline, students reading below 90% accuracy are likely to feel frustrated as they read. There are also a variety of published reading assessment tools that can be used to assess students' reading levels with the running record format.

- **Refer to other resources:** Other ways to determine instructional reading levels are to check your students' Individualized Education Plans, ask the school's ELL and special education teachers, or review test scores. All of these resources should be able to give you the further information you need to determine at which reading level to place a student.

Teachers can also use the texts in this series to scaffold the content for their students. At the beginning of the year, students at the lowest reading levels may need focused teacher guidance. As the year progresses, teachers can begin giving students multiple levels of the same text to allow them to work independently to improve their comprehension. This means each student would have a copy of the text at his or her independent reading level and instructional reading level. As students read the instructional-level texts, they can use the lower texts to better understand the difficult vocabulary. By scaffolding the content in this way, teachers can support students as they move up through the reading levels. This will encourage students to work with texts that are closer to the grade level at which they will be tested.

General Information About the Student Populations

Special Education Students

By Dennis Benjamin

Gone are the days of a separate special education curriculum. Federal government regulations require that special education students have access to the general education curriculum. For the vast majority of special education students today, their Individualized Education Plans (IEPs) contain current and targeted performance levels but few short-term content objectives. In other words, the special education students are required to learn the same content objectives as their regular education peers.

Be well aware of the accommodations and modifications written in students' IEPs. Use them in your teaching and assessment so they become routine. If you hold high expectations of success for all your students, their efforts and performances will rise as well. Remember the root word of *disability* is *ability*. Go to the root of the special needs learner and apply good teaching. The results will astound and please both of you.

English Language Learners

By Marcela von Vacano

Many school districts have chosen the inclusion model to integrate English language learners (ELLs) into mainstream classrooms. This model has its benefits as well as its drawbacks. One benefit is that English language learners may be able to learn from their peers by hearing and using English more frequently. One drawback is that these second-language learners cannot understand academic language and concepts without special instruction. They need sheltered instruction to take the first steps toward mastering English. In an inclusion classroom, the teacher may not have the time or necessary training to provide specialialized instruction for these learners.

Acquiring a second language is a lengthy process that integrates listening, speaking, reading, and writing. Students who are newcomers to the English language are not able to process information until they have mastered a certain number of structures and vocabulary words. Students may learn social language in one or two years. However, academic language takes up to eight years for most students.

Teaching academic language requires good planning and effective implementation. Pacing, or the rate at which information is presented, is another important component in this process. English language learners need to hear the same word in context several times, and they need to practice structures to internalize the words. Reviewing and summarizing what was taught are absolutely necessary for English language learners.

© *Shell Education*

General Information About the Student Populations *(cont.)*

English Language Learners *(cont.)*

Oral language proficiency is the first step in the language learning process. Oral language is defined as speaking and listening skills. English language learners are able to attain word-level skills (decoding, word recognition, and spelling) regardless of their oral-language proficiency. However, an ELL's ability to comprehend text and to develop writing skills is dependent on his or her oral-language proficiency. Therefore, "vocabulary knowledge, listening comprehension, syntactic skills and the ability to handle meta-linguistic aspects of language, such as being able to provide the definitions of words, are linked to English reading and writing proficiency" (August and Shanahan 2006). First-language oral proficiency has a positive impact on developmental patterns in second-language speech discrimination and production, intra-word segmentation, and vocabulary.

Regular Education Students

By Wendy Conklin

Often, regular education students get overlooked when planning curriculum. More emphasis is usually placed on those who struggle and, at times, on those who excel. Teachers spend time teaching basic skills and even go below grade level to ensure that all students are up to speed. While this is a noble thing and is necessary at times, in the midst of it all, the regular education students can get lost in the shuffle. We must not forget that differentiated strategies are good for the on-grade level students, too. Providing activities that are too challenging can frustrate these students, and on the other hand, assignments that are too easy can be boring and a waste of their time. The key to reaching this population successfully is to find just the right level of activities and questions while keeping a keen eye on their diverse learning styles.

There are many ways to differentiate for this population. Strategies can include designing activities based on the multiple intelligences theory. Current brain research points to the success of active learning strategies. These strategies provoke strong positive emotions and use movement during the learning process to help these students learn more effectively. Regular education students also benefit from direct teaching of higher-level thinking skills. Keep the activities open-ended so that these students can surprise you with all they know. The strategies described on pages 9–17 were specifically chosen because they are very effective for meeting the needs of regular education students as well as special populations.

General Information About the Student Populations (cont.)

Gifted Education Students

By Wendy Conklin

In recent years, many state and school district budgets have cut funding that has in the past provided resources for their gifted and talented programs. The push and focus of schools nationwide is proficiency. It is important that students have the basic skills to read fluently, solve math problems, and grasp scientific concepts. As a result, funding has been redistributed in hopes of improving test scores on state and national standardized tests. In many cases, the attention has focused only on improving low test scores to the detriment of the gifted students who need to be challenged.

Differentiating through the products you require from your students is a very effective and fairly easy way to meet the needs of gifted students. Actually, this simple change to your assignments will benefit all levels of students in your classroom. While some students are strong verbally, others express themselves better through nonlinguistic representation. After reading the texts in this book, students can express their comprehension through different means, such as drawings, plays, songs, skits, or videos. It is important to identify and address different learning styles. By assigning more open-ended assignments, you allow for more creativity and diversity in your classroom. These differentiated products can easily be aligned with content standards. To assess these standards, use differentiated rubrics.

All students should be learning, growing, and expanding their knowledge in school. This includes gifted students, too. But, they will not grow and learn unless someone challenges them with appropriate curriculum. Doing this can be overwhelming at times, even for the experienced teacher. However, there are some strategies that teachers can use to challenge the gifted population. These strategies include open-ended questions, student-directed learning, and using tiered assignments. (See pages 16–17 for more information about each of these strategies.)

Strategies for Using the Leveled Texts

Special Education Students

By Dennis Benjamin

KWL Chart

Too often, special education students fall prey to low expectations. In some classrooms, special education students even buy into this negative mentality. They begin to reply "I don't know" when they are asked any question. The **KWL** strategy empowers students to take back ownership over their learning. This strategy can be used as a prereading strategy with the texts in this book. **K** stands for What I *Know*. This first part of the process allows students to access prior knowledge and begin to make connections to the new learning about to take place. For example, when asked what they **K**now about immigrants, students will reply with responses such as Ellis Island, New York City, Angel Island, and potato famine.

The astute teacher praises the special needs students for how much they know about immigrants and challenges them with the What Do You *Want* to Know? column. Encourage the students to create meaningful questions that cannot be answered simply with yes or no. Initially, the teacher may model the questions, but ultimately students need to generate their own questions such as: *Why did they come to America?* and *What did they do when they arrived?* Now the students have set a purpose for reading nonfiction. The reading is no longer about what the teacher wants or expects. Inquisitive minds have been opened to discover what the texts have to offer.

The **L** is for What I *Learned*. After reading, the students should get back into a group to complete this third column. Students should then record the answers to the questions they wrote and any important concepts they learned from the text. Some students may benefit from identifying the source of information by writing such terms as *text*, *classroom talk*, or *homework* after each entry. That way, they can remember from where their answers came. Take the time to correct any misconceptions.

Once completed, it is important for the teacher to validate students' responses as they review the KWL chart. Praise the students for all the effort they put into the chart and highlight that they, as the learners, were responsible for its completeness and accuracy. This final step is important to help empower your special education students and encourage them to care more about their own learning.

Strategies for Using the Leveled Texts (cont.)

Special Education Students (cont.)

Vocabulary Scavenger Hunt

Another prereading strategy is a Vocabulary Scavenger Hunt. Students preview the text and highlight unknown words. Students then write the words on specially divided pages. The pages are divided into quarters with the following headings: *Definition*, *Sentence*, *Examples*, and *Nonexamples*. A section called *Picture* is put over the middle of the chart.

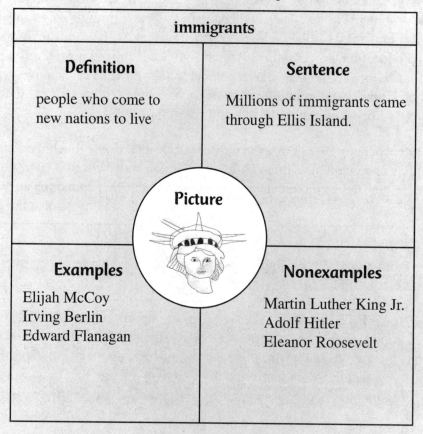

immigrants	
Definition people who come to new nations to live	**Sentence** Millions of immigrants came through Ellis Island.
Examples Elijah McCoy Irving Berlin Edward Flanagan	**Nonexamples** Martin Luther King Jr. Adolf Hitler Eleanor Roosevelt

This encounter with new vocabulary enables students to use it properly. The definition identifies the word's meaning in student-friendly language. The sentence should be written so that the word is used in context. This helps the student make connections with background knowledge. Illustrating the sentence gives a visual clue. Examples help students prepare for factual questions from the teacher or on standardized assessments. Nonexamples help students prepare for *not* and *except for* test questions such as "All of these are immigrants *except for . . .*" and "Which of these people is *not* an immigrant?" Any information the student was unable to record before reading can be added after reading the text.

10

© *Shell Education*

Strategies for Using the Leveled Texts (cont.)

Special Education Students (cont.)

Graphic Organizers to Find Similarities and Differences

Setting a purpose for reading content focuses the learner. One purpose for reading can be to identify similarities and differences. This is a skill that must be directly taught, modeled, and applied. The authors of *Classroom Instruction That Works* state that identifying similarities and differences "might be considered the core of all learning" (Marzano, Pickering, and Pollock 2001, 14). Higher-level tasks include comparing and classifying information and using metaphors and analogies. One way to scaffold these skills is through the use of graphic organizers, which help students focus on the essential information and organize their thoughts.

Example of Classifying Graphic Organizer

Immigrant	Country they left	Why they left	When they arrived	What they are known for
Elijah McCoy	Canada	to find work on locomotives	1870	creating the first lubricating cup
Madeleine Albright	Czechoslovakia	to escape Communist rule	1948	first female secretary of state
Irving Berlin	Russia	to escape pogroms	1893	composing famous songs
Ieoh Ming Pei	China	to study architecture	1935	famous world architect

The Riddles Graphic Organizer allows students to compare and contrast the explorers using riddles. Students first complete a chart you've designed. Then, using that chart, they can write summary sentences. They do this by using the riddle clues and reading across the chart. Students can also read down the chart and write summary sentences. With the chart below, students could write the following sentences: *McCoy and Berlin came during the 1800s. Albright and Pei came during the 1900s.*

Example of Riddles Graphic Organizer

Who Am I?	McCoy	Albright	Berlin	Pei
I came in the 1800s.	x		x	
I came in the 1900s.		x		x
I am a male.	x		x	x
I left to find work.	x			
I escaped terrible conditions.		x	x	

Strategies for Using the Leveled Texts (cont.)

Special Education Students (cont.)

Framed Outline

This is an underused technique that bears great results. Many special education students have problems with reading comprehension. They need a framework to help them attack the text and gain confidence in comprehending the material. Once students gain confidence and learn how to locate factual information, the teacher can fade out this technique.

There are two steps to successfully using this technique. First, the teacher writes cloze sentences. Second, the students complete the cloze activity and write summary sentences.

Example of Framed Outline

In the 1800s, _____ killed thousands of Jewish people in Europe. Irving _____'s family was one of these families. They fled _____ for New York City in 1893. They lived in the dark, dirty basement of a _____. The building was very overcrowded. _____ spread easily. As a result, Berlin's father died in _____.

Summary sentences: *Irving Berlin's family fled Europe. They moved to New York City. Berlin's father died young, and Berlin had to make money.*

Modeling Written Responses

A frequent criticism heard by special educators is that special education students write poor responses to content-area questions. This problem can be remedied if special education and classroom teachers model what good answers look like. While this may seem like common sense, few teachers take the time to do this. They just assume all children know how to respond in writing.

So, this is a technique you may want to use before asking your students to respond to the comprehension questions associated with the leveled texts in this series. First, read the question aloud. Then, write the question on an overhead and talk aloud about how you would go about answering the question. Next, write the answer using a complete sentence that accurately answers the question. Repeat the procedure for several questions so that students make the connection that quality written responses are your expectation.

As a warm-up activity, post a variety of responses to a single question. Ask students to identify the strongest responses and tell why they are strong. Have students identify the weakest answers and tell why they are weak. Ask for volunteers to come to the overhead and rewrite the weak responses so that they are strong. By doing this simple process, you are helping students evaluate and strengthen their own written responses.

© *Shell Education*

Strategies for Using the Leveled Texts *(cont.)*

English Language Learners

By Marcela von Vacano

Effective teaching for English language learners (ELLs) requires effective planning. In order to achieve success, teachers need to understand and use a conceptual framework to help them plan lessons and units. There are six major components to any framework. Each is described in more detail below.

1. **Select and Define Concepts and Language Objectives**—Before having students read one of the texts in this book, the teacher must first choose a social studies concept and language objective (reading, writing, listening, or speaking) appropriate for the grade level. Then, the next step is to clearly define the concept to be taught. This requires knowledge of the subject matter, alignment with local and state objectives, and careful formulation of a statement that defines the concept. This concept represents the overarching idea. The social studies concept should be written on paper and posted in a visible place in the classroom.

   By the definition of the concept, post a set of key language objectives. Based on the content and language objectives, select essential vocabulary from the text. The number of new words selected should be based on students' English language levels. Post these words on a word wall that may be arranged alphabetically or by themes.

2. **Build Background Knowledge**—Some ELLs may have a lot of knowledge in their native language, while others may have little or no knowledge. The teacher will want to build the background knowledge of the students using different strategies such as the following:

   Visuals—Use posters, photographs, postcards, newspapers, magazines, drawings, and video clips of the topic you are presenting. The texts in this series include multiple primary sources for your use.

   Realia—Bring real-life objects to the classroom. If you are teaching about World War II, bring in items such as letters or photographs.

   Vocabulary and Word Wall—Introduce key vocabulary in context. Create families of words. Have students draw pictures that illustrate the words and write sentences about the words. Also be sure you have posted the words on a word wall in your classroom.

   Desk Dictionaries—Have students create their own desk dictionaries using index cards. On one side, they should draw a picture of the word. On the opposite side, they should write the word in their own language and in English.

Strategies for Using the Leveled Texts *(cont.)*

English Language Learners *(cont.)*

3. **Teach Concepts and Language Objectives**—The teacher must present content and language objectives clearly. He or she must engage students by using a hook and must pace the delivery of instruction, taking into consideration the students' English language levels. The concept or concepts to be taught must be stated clearly. Use the first languages of the students whenever possible or assign other students who speak the same languages to mentor and to work cooperatively with the ELLs.

   Lev Semenovich Vygotsky, a Russian psychologist, wrote about the Zone of Proximal Development (ZPD). This theory states that good instruction must fill the gap that exists between the present knowledge of a child and the child's potential. Scaffolding instruction is an important component when planning and teaching lessons. ELLs cannot jump stages of language and content development. You must determine where the students are in the learning process and teach to the next level using several small steps to get to the desired outcome. With the leveled texts in this series and periodic assessment of students' language levels, teachers can support students as they climb the academic ladder.

4. **Practice Concepts and Language Objectives**—ELLs need to practice what they learn through engaging activities. Most people retain knowledge best after applying what they learn to their own lives. This is definitely true for English language learners. Students can apply content and language knowledge by creating projects, stories, skits, poems, or artifacts that show what they learned. Some activities should be geared to the right side of the brain, like those listed above. For students who are left-brain dominant, activities such as defining words and concepts, using graphic organizers, and explaining procedures should be developed. The following teaching strategies are effective in helping students practice both language and content:

   Simulations—Students recreate history by becoming a part of it. They have to make decisions as if they lived in historical times. For example, students can pretend that they are traveling to the United States as immigrants. They have to figure out where they will arrive and what they will choose to take with them on their trips. First, they need to brainstorm ideas, and then they can get the actual objects and put them in small bags. Lastly, they present their objects to the class and give explanations for why they chose each item.

#50084—*Leveled Texts: The 20th Century* © *Shell Education*

Strategies for Using the Leveled Texts *(cont.)*

English Language Learners *(cont.)*

4. Practice Concepts and Language Objectives *(cont.)*

Literature response—Read a text from this book. Have students choose two people described or introduced in the text. Ask students to create a conversation the people might have. Or, you can have students write journal entries about events in the daily lives of the historic people.

Have a short debate—Make a controversial statement such as, *"Germany was treated unfairly after World War I."* After reading a text in this book, have students think about the question and take a position. As students present their ideas, one student can act as a moderator.

Interview—Students may interview a member of the family or a neighbor in order to obtain information regarding a topic from the texts in this book. For example: *What was it like to live during the Great Depression?*

5. Evaluation and Alternative Assessments—We know that evaluation is used to inform instruction. Students must have opportunities to show their understanding of concepts in different ways and not only through standard assessments. Use both formative and summative assessments to ensure that you are effectively meeting your content and language objectives. Formative assessment is used to plan effective lessons for a particular group of students. Summative assessment is used to find out how much the students have learned. Other authentic assessments that show day-to-day progress are: text retelling, teacher rating scales, students self-evaluations, cloze testing, holistic scoring of writing samples, performance assessments, and portfolios. Periodically assessing student learning will help you ensure that students continue to receive the correct levels of texts.

6. Home-School Connection—The home-school connection is an important component in the learning process for ELLs. Parents are the first teachers, and they establish expectations for their children. These expectations help shape the behavior of their children. By asking parents to be active participants in the education of their children, students get a double dose of support and encouragement. As a result, families become partners in the education of their children and the chances for success in your classroom increase.

You can send home copies of the texts in this series for parents to read with their children. You can even send multiple levels to meet the needs of your second-language parents as well as your students. In this way, you are sharing your social studies content standards with your whole second-language community.

Strategies for Using the Leveled Texts *(cont.)*

Gifted Education Students

By Wendy Conklin

Open-Ended Questions and Activities

Teachers need to be aware of activities that provide a ceiling that is too low for gifted students. When given activities like this, gifted students become bored. We know these students can do more, but how much more? Offering open-ended questions and activities will give high-ability students the opportunities to perform at or above their ability levels. For example, ask students to evaluate major events described in the texts, such as: *"Would you have sided with President Wilson about the war?"* or *"Would you have wanted to join World War I?"* These questions require students to form opinions, think deeply about the issues, and form pro and con statements in their minds. To questions like this, there really is not one right answer.

The generic open-ended question stems listed below can be adapted to any topic. There is one leveled comprehension question for each text in this book. The question stems below can be used to develop further comprehension questions for the leveled texts.

- In what ways did . . .
- How might you have done this differently . . .
- What if . . .
- What are some possible explanations for . . .
- How does this affect . . .
- Explain several reasons why . . .
- What problems does this create . . .
- Describe the ways . . .
- What is the best . . .
- What is the worst . . .
- What is the likelihood . . .
- Predict the outcome . . .
- Form a hypothesis . . .
- What are three ways to classify . . .
- Support your reason . . .
- Compare this to modern times . . .
- Make a plan for . . .
- Propose a solution . . .
- What is an alternative to . . .

© *Shell Education*

Strategies for Using the Leveled Texts (cont.)

Gifted Education Students (cont.)

Student-Directed Learning

Because they are academically advanced, gifted students are often the leaders in classrooms. They are more self-sufficient learners, too. As a result, there are some student-directed strategies that teachers can employ successfully with these students. Remember to use the texts in this book as jumpstarts so that students will be interested in finding out more about the time periods. Gifted students may enjoy any of the following activities:

- Writing their own questions, exchanging their questions with others, and grading the responses.
- Reviewing the lesson and teaching the topic to another group of students.
- Reading other nonfiction texts about this time period to further expand their knowledge.
- Writing the quizzes and tests to go along with the texts.
- Creating illustrated time lines to be displayed as visuals for the entire class.
- Putting together multimedia presentations using primary sources from the time period.
- Leading discussion groups about the texts or time periods.
- Researching topics from the texts in depth and writing new texts on these topics.

Tiered Assignments

Teachers can differentiate lessons by using tiered assignments, or scaffolded lessons. Tiered assignments are parallel tasks designed to have varied levels of depth, complexity, and abstractness. All students work toward one goal, concept, or outcome, but the lesson is tiered to allow for different levels of readiness and performance levels. As students work, they build on their prior knowledge and understanding. Students are motivated to be successful according to their own readiness and learning preferences.

Guidelines for writing tiered lessons include the following:

1. Pick the skill, concept, or generalization that needs to be learned.
2. Think of an on-grade-level activity that teaches this skill, concept, or generalization.
3. Assess the students using classroom discussions, quizzes, tests, or journal entries and place them in groups.
4. Take another look at the activity from Step 2. Modify this activity to meet the needs of the below-grade-level and above-grade-level learners in the class. Add complexity and depth for the gifted students. Add vocabulary support and concrete examples for the below-grade-level students.

17

How to Use This Product

Readability Chart

Title of the Text	Star	Circle	Square	Triangle
The Industrial Revolution	2.1	3.2	5.0	6.7
Men of the Industrial Revolution	2.0	3.2	4.8	6.5
European Immigration	2.0	3.3	4.9	6.5
Asian Immigration	2.0	3.3	4.7	6.8
World War I: The "Great War"	2.2	3.1	4.8	6.8
The Roaring Twenties	1.8	3.2	4.5	6.5
The Great Depression	1.6	3.1	4.6	6.5
World War II in Europe	2.0	3.0	4.6	6.5
World War II in the Pacific	2.0	3.0	4.5	6.6
World War II Leaders	2.2	3.2	4.7	6.9
The Civil Rights Movement	2.2	3.0	4.7	6.5
Dr. Martin Luther King Jr.	2.2	3.0	4.7	6.6
The Cold War	2.0	3.0	5.1	6.5
Conflicts in the Middle East	2.2	3.1	5.2	6.5
Modern World Leaders	2.2	3.2	5.0	6.6

Correlation to Standards

The No Child Left Behind (NCLB) legislation mandates that all states adopt academic standards that identify the skills students will learn in kindergarten through grade 12. While many states had already adopted academic standards prior to NCLB, the legislation set requirements to ensure the standards were detailed and comprehensive. In many states today, teachers are required to demonstrate how their lessons meet state standards. State standards are used in the development of Shell Education products, so educators can be assured that they meet the academic requirements of each state.

Shell Education is committed to producing educational materials that are research and standards based. In this effort, all products are correlated to the academic standards of the 50 states, the District of Columbia, and the Department of Defense Dependent Schools. A correlation report customized for your state can be printed directly from the following website: **http://www.shelleducation.com**. If you require assistance in printing correlation reports, please contact Customer Service at 1-877-777-3450.

McREL Compendium

Shell Education uses the Mid-continent Research for Education and Learning (McREL) Compendium to create standards correlations. Each year, McREL analyzes state standards and revises the compendium. By following this procedure, they are able to produce a general compilation of national standards. The social studies standards on which the texts in this book focus are correlated to state standards at **http://www.shelleducation.com**.

How to Use This Product (cont.)

Components of the Product

Primary Sources

- Each level of text includes multiple primary sources. These documents, photographs, and illustrations add interest to the texts. The historical images also serve as visual support for second language learners. They make the texts more context rich and bring the texts to life.

Comprehension Questions

- Each level of text includes one comprehension question. Like the texts, the comprehension questions were leveled by an expert. They are written to allow all students to be successful within a whole-class discussion. The questions for the same topic are closely linked so that the teacher can ask a question on that topic and all students will be able to answer it. The lowest-level students might focus on the facts, while the upper-level students can delve deeper into the meanings.

- Teachers may want to base their whole-class question on the square level questions. Those were the starting points for all the other leveled questions.

The Levels

- There are 15 topics in this book. Each topic is leveled to four different reading levels. The images and fonts used for each level within a topic look the same.

- Behind each page number, you'll see a shape. These shapes indicate the reading levels of each piece so that you can make sure students are working with the correct texts. The reading levels fall into the ranges indicated to the left. See the chart on page 18 for specific levels of each text.

Leveling Process

- The texts in this series are taken from the Primary Source Readers kits published by Teacher Created Materials. A reading expert went through the texts and leveled each one to create four distinct reading levels.

- After that, a special education expert and an English language learner expert carefully reviewed the lowest two levels and suggested changes that would help their students comprehend the texts better.

- The texts were then leveled one final time to ensure the editorial changes made during the process kept them within the ranges described to the left.

Levels
1.5–2.2

Levels
3.0–3.5

Levels
4.5–5.2

Levels
6.5–7.2

© Shell Education

#50084–Leveled Texts: The 20th Century

How to Use This Product (cont.)

Tips for Managing the Product

How to Prepare the Texts

- When you copy these texts, be sure you set your copier to copy photographs. Run a few test pages and adjust the contrast, as necessary. If you want the students to be able to appreciate the images, you need to carefully prepare the texts for them.

- You also have full-color versions of the texts provided in PDF form on the CD. (See page 144 for more information.) Depending on how many copies you need to make, printing the full-color versions and copying those might work best for you.

- Keep in mind that you should copy two-sided to two-sided if you pull the pages out of the book. The shapes behind the page numbers will help you keep the pages organized as you prepare them.

Distributing the Texts

- Some teachers wonder about how to hand the texts out within one classroom. They worry that students will feel insulted if they do not get the same papers as their neighbors. The first step in dealing with these texts is to set up your classroom as a place where all students learn at their individual instructional levels. Making this clear as a fact of life in your classroom is key. Otherwise, the students may constantly ask about why their work is different. You do not need to get into the technicalities of the reading levels. Just state it as a fact that every student will not be working on the same assignment every day. If you do this, then passing out the varied levels is not a problem. Just hand them to the correct students as you circle the room.

- If you would rather not have students openly aware of the differences in the texts, you can try these ways to pass out the materials.

  - Make a pile in your hands from star to triangle. Put your finger between the circle and square levels. As you approach each student, you pull from the top (star), above your finger (circle), below your finger (square), or the bottom (triangle). If you do not hesitate too much in front of each desk, the students will probably not notice.

  - Begin the class period with an opening activity. Put the texts in different places around the room. As students work quietly, circulate and direct students to the right locations for retrieving the texts you want them to use.

  - Organize the texts in small piles by seating arrangement so that when you arrive at a group of desks, you have just the levels you need.

20

© *Shell Education*

The Industrial Revolution

In the 1700s, a great change began. The change started in Great Britain. People stopped making things by hand. Machines made things. Factories were built. Banks opened. It was the Industrial Revolution (in-DUHS-tree-uhl rev-uh-LOO-shuhn). Making things by machine changed the world.

In America, steel was like gold. Why? Steel can be made into almost anything. Machines and ships are made of steel. So are bridges and railroad tracks. Trains move across land on steel. The railroads made it easy to move goods. Canals, or waterways, let boats move things, too.

Machines changed the textile (TEKS-tile), or cloth, business. Before this, people had spun thread. They used the thread to weave cloth. Then they made clothes. They did all this by hand. They did it in their homes. Now, machines did these jobs. The machines made things faster. More goods were made. The nation's economy (ih-KAWN-uh-mee) grew. The economy is based on the amount of goods and services a country makes. The more goods made, the more the economy grew. Businesses could charge less money for their goods. So, more people could buy more things. People in other nations bought the things, too.

Take Me to the Bank!

Banks brought together people who save money and industrialists (in-DUHS-tree-uhl-istz). These men owned companies. People put their cash in banks. The banks paid them interest. So, savers got money for putting their cash in the bank. They earned one percent (1%). The banks lent out the cash. A man could use it to start or add to his business. Later, he had to pay back the bank. He gave back the cash. And he paid three percent (3%) interest. So, the banks made money. How? They got more money back than they paid out in interest. Banking helped the banks, the savers, and the business owners.

To get cash, or capital, some companies sold stocks. Stocks are part ownership in a company. Let's say a person gave cash to a business owner for some stock. Then, he owned a small part of the business. That meant that he would get a little of the profits. Profits are the money made by the business.

21

Trust Busting

A few companies wanted to run everything. First, a company bought up the other companies in its business. Then, it made trusts. A trust is when one company runs everything. So, in 1890, the Sherman Antitrust Act was made a law. It said there could be no trusts. It said there could be no monopolies (muh-NAWP-uh-leez) either. A monopoly is when one company is in charge of all of an industry.

Labor Unions

Business owners gave workers low pay. They made them work long hours. The people worked in dirty and unsafe places. So the workers started labor unions. Workers in a labor union stood together. They asked for what they needed. If the owner did not listen, they went on strike. If all the workers went on strike, the business could not run.

In 1827, Philadelphia builders worked 12 hours a day. It was too much. They went on strike. Other workers did, too. It worked! Unions got a 10-hour workday for workers.

Muckrakers Check Out Big Businesses

Muckrakers were writers. They looked into businesses. They wrote about what they found. One writer was Upton Sinclair. He wrote about meat-packing plants. There, people turned cows and pigs into food. They worked in bad settings. A grinder chopped up a man's finger. His flesh went into the meat. It was sent out for people to eat! Mr. Sinclair let people know this. People thought about how workers should be treated. Labor unions grew stronger. New laws passed. Things got better for workers.

Comprehension Question

How did machines change the textile business?

© Shell Education

The Industrial Revolution

In the 1700s, a great change began. The change started in Great Britain. People no longer made all things by hand. Instead, machines did the work. Factories were built. Banks opened. This time is called the Industrial Revolution (in-DUHS-tree-uhl rev-uh-LOO-shuhn). Making things by machine changed the world.

American companies grew because of steel. Steel can be made into almost anything. By 1860, steel was used to make machines and ships. It built bridges and railroad tracks. Railroads went across the nation because of steel. Railroads made it fast and easy to move things. Canals, or waterways, let boats move goods, too.

Machines changed the textile (TEKS-tile), or cloth, industry, too. Before, people had spun thread. They used the thread to weave cloth. Then they made clothes by hand. They did all this in their homes. Now, factories did these jobs. Machines let workers make products fast. The more goods made, the more the nation's economy (ih-KAWN-uh-mee) grew. The economy is based on the worth of the goods and services a country makes. Businesses could charge less for their goods. So, more people could buy more things. People in other nations bought the things, too.

Take Me to the Bank!

Banks brought together people who save money and industrialists (in-DUHS-tree-uhl-istz). These men owned businesses. People took their cash to banks. The banks gave them interest. The rate was one percent (1%). Interest is what people got for putting their cash in banks. Then, the banks lent out the cash to start or add to a business. Over time, the borrower had to pay back the bank. He paid back the loan amount and three percent (3%) interest. The banks made money. How? They got more money back than they paid out in interest.

To get cash, or capital, some companies sold stocks. Stocks are part ownership in a company. A person gave cash to the business owner. In return, the person owned a small part of the business. That meant that he would get a little bit of the profits. The more stock he bought, the more of the business he owned.

23

Trust Busting

Some companies wanted to run everything. First, a company bought most of the businesses just like it. Then, it created trusts. This forced the others to limit production and kept prices low. In effect, a trust let one company run the whole industry. So in 1890, the Sherman Antitrust Act was passed. It banned monopolies (muh-NAWP-uh-leez). A monopoly is when one person or company has total control of a market or industry. The act stated that no company could make a trust.

Labor Unions

Most business owners did not care about workers. They had them work long hours. They gave them low pay. The people worked in hot, dirty, and unsafe places. So, the workers formed labor unions. Workers in a labor union agreed to stand together. Sometimes, they went on strike. This means they all decided to not work. They did this to make sure they were treated fairly. If all the workers went on strike, the factory could not run.

In 1827, Philadelphia carpenters worked 12 hours each day. They wanted to work less. They went on strike. Other workers did, too. Working conditions got better for these workers. Soon, other groups did the same. In this way, unions got a 10-hour workday to be standard by the 1850s.

Muckrakers Target Big Businesses

Muckrakers, or writers, looked into businesses. Then, they wrote about what they found. One famous muckraker was Upton Sinclair. In his book called *The Jungle,* he wrote about meat-packing plants. There, people turned cows and pigs into food. They worked in filthy conditions. One man had his finger chopped up by a grinder. His flesh went into the sausage. It was sent out for people to eat! Muckrakers got people to think. They thought about working conditions and how people ought to be treated. This let labor unions grow stronger. New laws passed. Working conditions got better.

Comprehension Question

In what ways did machines change the lives of textile workers?

The Industrial Revolution

In the 1700s, a great change began in Great Britain. It marked the end of people making everything by hand. Instead, machines did the work. Factories were built and banks opened. This time is called the Industrial Revolution (in-DUHS-tree-uhl rev-uh-LOO-shuhn), and it changed the world forever.

American industry grew due to the increased use of steel. Steel can be formed into almost anything. By 1860, it was used for machines, ships, bridges, and railroad tracks. Steel allowed railroads to spread across the nation. Railroads made it fast and easy to move items. Canals were dug so that boats could move goods, too.

Machines changed the textile (TEKS-tile), or cloth, industry. Before, people had spun thread, woven cloth, and made clothes by hand in their homes. Now, these tasks moved into factories. Using machines, workers made products faster. The increased production made the nation's economy (ih-KAWN-uh-mee) grow. Businesses could charge less for their products. Then, more people could buy them. Sales were booming.

Take Me to the Bank!

Banks brought savers and industrialists (in-DUHS-tree-uhl-istz) together. People took their cash to banks. The banks gave them an interest rate of one percent. This means people earned money by putting their money in the banks. Then, the banks lent out the money to start or enlarge businesses. Over time, the borrowers had to pay back the banks. They paid back the original amount plus three percent interest. The banks made money because they got more money back than they paid out in interest.

To raise capital, some companies issued stocks. Stocks are part ownership in a company. A person gave the business owner cash. In return, he owned a small part of the business. That meant that he would get a little bit of the profits. The more stock he held, the greater his ownership in the business.

Trust Busting

Some companies wanted to control everything. First, a company bought most of its competitors. Then, it created trusts to force the others to limit production and keep prices low. In effect, a trust let one company "own" the whole industry. So, the Sherman Antitrust Act was passed in 1890. It banned monopolies (muh-NAWP-uh-leez). A monopoly is when one person or company has total control of a market or industry. The act also stated that no company could form a trust.

Labor Unions

Most business owners showed no concern for their workers. They had them work long hours for low pay in hot, dirty, and unsafe conditions. So, the workers formed labor unions. In a labor union, a group of workers agreed to stand together. Sometimes, they went on strike to make sure they were treated fairly. If all the workers went on strike, production came to a halt.

In 1827, Philadelphia carpenters worked 12-hour days, but they wanted to work fewer hours each day. They went on strike. Bricklayers and printers did, too. Working conditions improved for all three groups. Soon other groups did the same. Unions managed to get a 10-hour workday to be standard by the 1850s.

Muckrakers Target Big Businesses

Muckrakers investigated businesses. Then, they wrote about what they discovered. One famous muckraker was Upton Sinclair. In his book, *The Jungle,* he described meat-packing plants. There, people prepared cows and pigs for food in filthy conditions. One man had his finger destroyed by the grinder. His flesh went into the sausage. It was packaged and sent out for people to eat! Muckrakers got people to think about working conditions and how people ought to be treated. As a result, labor unions grew stronger. New laws were passed to help improve working conditions.

Comprehension Question

Describe at least three ways machines changed life during the Industrial Revolution.

The Industrial Revolution

In the 1700s, a great change began in Great Britain that marked the end of people making everything by hand. Instead, machines did the work. Factories were built and banks opened. This time is called the Industrial Revolution (in-DUHS-tree-uhl rev-uh-LOO-shuhn), and it changed the world dramatically.

American industry grew rapidly due to the increased use of steel. Steel can be formed into almost anything. By 1860, it was used for machines, ships, bridges, and railroad tracks. Steel allowed railroads to spread across the nation. Railroads made it fast and easy to transport items. Canals were dug so that boats could transport goods, too.

Machines also changed the textile (TEKS-tile), or cloth, industry. Before, people had spun thread, woven cloth, and made clothes by hand in their homes. Now, these tasks moved into factories. Machines let workers make many products rapidly. Increased production made the nation's economy (ih-KAWN-uh-mee) grow. Businesses could charge less for their products, and more people could buy them. Sales were exploding.

Take Me to the Bank!

Banks brought savers and industrialists (in-DUHS-tree-uhl-istz) together. People took their cash to banks because the banks paid them an interest rate of one percent. People liked the fact that they earned money by keeping their funds in the banks. Then, the banks lent entrepreneurs the money they needed to start or enlarge businesses. After a period of time, the borrowers had to pay back the banks the original amount plus three percent interest. The banks made money because they got more money back than they paid out in interest. In this way, the industrialists, the savers, and the bankers all profited.

Some companies issued stocks as a way to get capital. Stocks are part ownership in a company. A person gave the business owner cash, and in return, he got a certificate stating that he owned a small part of the business and would get a little bit of the profits. The more stock a person held, the greater his ownership in the business.

27

Trust Busting

Some companies wanted to control everything. First, a company bought most of its competitors. Then, it created trusts to force the others to limit production and keep prices low. In effect, a trust let one company "own" the whole industry until the Sherman Antitrust Act was passed in 1890. It banned monopolies (muh-NAWP-uh-leez) and stated that no company could form a trust. A monopoly is when one person or company has total control of a market or industry.

Labor Unions

Most entrepreneurs showed no concern for their workers. They had them work long hours for low pay in hot, dirty, and dangerous conditions. So, the workers formed labor unions. In a labor union, a group of workers agreed to stand together. Sometimes, they went on strike to make sure they were treated fairly. If all the workers went on strike, production in a factory came to a halt.

In 1827, Philadelphia carpenters worked 12-hour days, but they wanted to work a 10-hour day instead. To change this they went on strike. Bricklayers and printers did, too. As a result, working conditions improved for all three groups, and soon other groups did the same. Unions managed to get a 10-hour workday to be standard by the 1850s.

Muckrakers Target Big Businesses

Muckrakers investigated businesses and wrote about their discoveries. One famous muckraker was Upton Sinclair. In his book, *The Jungle*, he described meat-packing plants where people made food in filthy conditions. A grinder destroyed one man's finger, and his flesh went into the sausage. It was packaged and sent out for people to consume! Muckrakers got people thinking about working conditions and how laborers should be treated. As a result, labor unions grew stronger, and new laws improved working conditions.

Comprehension Question

In what ways did machines help the American economy during the Industrial Revolution?

© Shell Education

Men of the Industrial Revolution

During the Industrial Revolution (in-DUHS-tree-uhl rev-uh-LOO-shuhn), inventors made up new things. Then, businesses made a lot of each invention. Bankers lent cash to companies. Companies grew bigger. The three largest American businesses sold steel, oil, and cars.

A Man of Steel

In 1847, Andrew Carnegie was 12 years old. He came to the United States from Scotland. When he was 17, a railroad executive (ig-ZEK-yuh-tiv) chose him to work for him. This man helped to run the Pennsylvania Railroad. He made brave choices. He chose Andrew Carnegie to help him in the railroad business. Carnegie learned to act fast. He made bold choices.

Andrew Carnegie left the railroad. He opened a big steel mill. He was wise. His steel mill company grew and grew. His business grew even when other steel mills did not do well. Andrew Carnegie bought more steel mills. He retired in 1901. He sold the Carnegie Steel Company. It sold for $480 million.

An Oil Tycoon

In 1839, John D. Rockefeller was born in New York. As a child, he worked for a farmer. He got 35 cents a day. When he was 10, John Rockefeller had $50. He lent his cash to a man. The man paid it back. He paid it back with interest. This means he paid extra money. The man gave back more cash than he had borrowed. John Rockefeller was glad. Rockefeller knew that he would go into business someday.

By the age of 22, John Rockefeller had saved a lot of cash. He used the money to help to build an oil company. The oil company drilled oil wells. It had a refinery. The refinery made the oil

© Shell Education

#50084—Leveled Texts: The 20th Century

ready for use. Because it was near water and the railroad, it was easy to move the oil. Three years passed. John Rockefeller bought his partners' stock. Then, he owned the whole company.

Later, John Rockefeller and some new partners started a new business. It was Standard Oil Company. It was the world's biggest refinery. It saved time and money. So, the cost of refining, or preparing, oil dropped. John Rockefeller bought oil fields, oil tank cars, and oil pipelines. He was one of the richest men of his time.

Born to Be a Banker

J. P. Morgan was born in 1837. His dad was a banker. When Morgan grew up, he worked for his dad. Soon, he knew all about banking. He started his own bank in 1862. J. P. Morgan knew which businesses would grow. He made sure he lent them money. People in Europe trusted him. They gave Morgan cash to spend to make the companies bigger. He used it to build U.S. businesses. The people who gave him cash earned profits and became richer.

Mr. Morgan became a financier (fih-nan-SUHR) for big companies. That means he loaned these companies money. At one time, he controlled banks and railroads. He was in charge of insurance companies and shipping lines. He was powerful. Some people thought that J. P. Morgan would take over the nation.

The Assembly Line Is Born

Henry Ford was born in Michigan in 1863. At age 16, Ford took a job at a machine shop. Then, he worked for a big shipbuilder. He learned all about motors. In 1903, Ford and two partners formed Ford Motor Company. They made cars. But the cars cost a lot. Only the rich could buy them. In 1908, Ford made the Model T. It cost less than other cars. More than 10,000 sold in the first year. The company could not make cars fast enough!

Then, Henry Ford had an idea. He invented the assembly line. Men stood along a conveyor (kuhn-VAY-uhr) belt. The belt moved slowly. On the conveyor belt was an engine. As the engine went past, each worker added parts to it. Things sped up. The cost to make a car went down. So, Ford cut the price. Soon, most people could buy a car!

Comprehension Question

What is a financier?

30

Men of the Industrial Revolution

During the Industrial Revolution (in-DUHS-tree-uhl rev-uh-LOO-shuhn), inventors created new items. Then, businesses made them in large amounts. Bankers lent money to companies. These companies grew bigger. The largest American businesses sold steel, oil, and cars.

A Man of Steel

Andrew Carnegie was 12 years old when he came to the United States in 1847. When he was 17, a railroad executive (ig-ZEK-yuh-tiv) noticed him. Andrew Carnegie became involved in running the Pennsylvania Railroad. He learned to act fast and make bold choices.

Andrew Carnegie left the railroad business in 1865. He opened a huge, modern steel mill. He made such wise decisions that his company grew and grew. Even when the nation's economy was not good, his business grew. Andrew Carnegie bought other steel mills. When he retired in 1901, he sold the Carnegie Steel Company for $480 million.

An Oil Tycoon

In 1839, John D. Rockefeller was born in New York. As a child, he worked for a farmer. He was paid 35 cents a day. By the age of 10, John Rockefeller had $50 saved in a jar. He lent this money to a man. The man paid it back with interest. He was paid his $50 plus $5. At that moment, Rockefeller knew that he would go into business.

By the time John Rockefeller turned 22, he had saved a lot of money. He helped to build Excelsior (ik-SELL-see-or) Oil Company. This company drilled oil wells and had a refinery. The refinery made the oil ready to use. The refinery was near water and the railroad. This made it easy to move the oil. After just three years, John Rockefeller bought his partners' stock. Then, he owned the whole company.

In 1870, Rockefeller and some new partners started Standard Oil Company. It was soon the world's biggest refinery. This refinery saved time and money. So, the cost of refining oil dropped. John Rockefeller used it to buy other refineries, oil fields, oil tank cars, and oil pipelines. He was one of the richest men of his time.

Born to Be a Banker

J. P. Morgan was born in 1837. His dad was a banker. When Morgan grew up, he worked for his dad. He soon knew all about banking. He went out on his own in 1862. He could tell which businesses would grow. He made sure he lent money to them. People in Europe trusted him. They gave him money to invest. He used the money to build American businesses. The people who had given him money earned profits.

J. P. Morgan became the main financier (fih-nan-SUHR) for big companies. That means he loaned these companies a lot of money. He controlled banks and railroads. He was in charge of insurance companies and shipping lines. He was powerful. Some people thought that he wanted to take over the whole country.

The Assembly Line Is Born

Henry Ford was born in Michigan in 1863. At age 16, Ford took a job at a machine shop. Then, he went to work for a large shipbuilder. He learned all about motors. In 1903, Ford and two partners formed Ford Motor Company. They made cars. But, their cars cost a lot. Only rich people could buy them. In 1908, Ford brought out the Model T. It was popular and cost less than other cars. More than 10,000 cars sold in the first year. The Ford Motor Company could not meet the demand.

Then, Henry Ford had an idea. He invented the assembly line. Men stood along a conveyor (kuhn-VAY-uhr) belt. As an engine moved past, each worker did one job. This sped up the process. The cost to make a car dropped. So, Ford cut the price. Soon, most people could have a car! The era of the car had arrived.

Comprehension Question

How did J. P. Morgan learn about the banking business?

#50084— *Leveled Texts: The 20th Century*

© Shell Education

Men of the Industrial Revolution

During the Industrial Revolution (in-DUHS-tree-uhl rev-uh-LOO-shuhn), inventors created new items. Then, businesses made them in great quantities. Bankers lent money to help companies grow. Soon, the biggest businesses sold steel, oil, and cars.

A Man of Steel

Andrew Carnegie was 12 years old when he came to the United States in 1847. When Carnegie was 17, a railroad executive (ig-ZEK-yuh-tiv) noticed him. Soon, Carnegie became involved in operating the Pennsylvania Railroad.

Carnegie left the railroad business in 1865 in order to open a large, modern steel mill. He made wise decisions. So, even when the economy dipped, his company kept growing. Carnegie bought other steel mills as well. When he retired in 1901, he sold the Carnegie Steel Company for $480 million.

An Oil Tycoon

In 1839, John D. Rockefeller was born on a farm in New York. As a child, he worked for a farmer for 35 cents a day. By the age of 10, Rockefeller had $50 in a jar. A man borrowed this money and repaid it with interest. At that moment, Rockefeller knew that he would go into business.

By the time Rockefeller turned 22, he had saved enough money to help build Excelsior (ik-SELL-see-or) Oil Company. The company drilled oil and had a refinery. Since it was near rail and water transportation, it was convenient to transport the oil. After only three years, Rockefeller bought all his partners' stock and owned the entire company.

In 1870, Rockefeller and some new partners started Standard Oil Company. It was soon the world's biggest refinery. This refinery saved time and money. Because of these savings, the cost of refining oil decrease. Rockefeller bought other refineries, oil fields, oil tank cars, and oil pipelines until he became one of the richest men of his time.

Born to Be a Banker

J. P. Morgan was born in 1837. When Morgan grew up, he worked for his father, who was a banker. Morgan soon knew all about banking and struck out on his own in 1862. He had a knack for knowing which industries would grow. He made sure he lent money to those businesses. Europeans gave him money to invest. He used it to build American companies. The investors earned profits.

Morgan became the financier (fih-nan-SUHR) for large companies. That means he loaned the companies a lot of money. At the height of his career, he controlled banks, railroads, insurance companies, and shipping lines. He was so powerful that some people worried that he wanted to take control of the whole country.

The Assembly Line Is Born

Henry Ford was born in Michigan in 1863. At age 16, Ford walked to Detroit and took a job at a machine shop. Then, he went to work for a large shipbuilder. He learned all about motors. In 1903, Ford and two partners formed Ford Motor Company in order to make cars. But, their cars cost so much that only rich people could afford to purchase them. In 1908, Ford brought out the Model T. It was very popular and less expensive than prior cars. More than 10,000 cars were sold the first year, and Ford Motor Company could not keep up with the demand.

Then, Ford had an idea. He invented the assembly line. Men stood along a conveyor (kuhn-VAY-uhr) belt. As an engine moved past, each worker did one job. This sped up the process. As the cost to make a car dropped, Ford cut the price. Soon, most people could afford a car! The era of the car had arrived.

Comprehension Question

How did J. P. Morgan make money by lending money?

#50084— *Leveled Texts: The 20th Century*

© Shell Education

Men of the Industrial Revolution

During the Industrial Revolution (in-DUHS-tree-uhl rev-uh-LOO-shuhn), inventors created new items which businesses then produced in great quantities. Bankers lent money to help companies grow bigger. The largest American industries sold steel, oil, and automobiles.

A Man of Steel

Andrew Carnegie was 12 years old when he arrived in the United States in 1847. When Carnegie was just 17, a railroad executive (ig-ZEK-yuh-tiv) noticed him, and he became involved in operating the Pennsylvania Railroad. He learned to act quickly and make bold decisions.

Carnegie left the railroad business in 1865 to open a huge, modern steel mill. He made such clever decisions that even when the nation's economy dipped, his company kept growing. Carnegie bought other steel mills. When he retired in 1901, he sold the Carnegie Steel Company for $480 million.

An Oil Tycoon

In 1839, John D. Rockefeller was born in New York. As a child, he worked for a farmer for 35 cents a day. Rockefeller saved this money and by the age of 10, he had $50 in a jar. A man borrowed the money and paid it back with interest. That's when Rockefeller knew that he would go into business.

By the time Rockefeller turned 22, he had saved enough money to help build Excelsior (ik-SELL-see-or) Oil Company. This company drilled oil, had a refinery, and was near rail and water transportation. This made it convenient to transport the refined oil. After just three years, Rockefeller bought his partners' stock in the business and took over the whole company.

In 1870, Rockefeller and some new partners started Standard Oil Company, which soon became the world's biggest refinery. He continually found ways to make the refinery function better, and the cost of refining oil decreased. Rockefeller bought other refineries, oil fields, oil tank cars, and oil pipelines until he became one of the wealthiest men of his time.

Born to Be a Banker

J. P. Morgan was born in 1837. When he grew up, he worked for his father, who was a banker. Soon, Morgan knew all about banking and struck out on his own in 1862. He had a knack for recognizing which industries would grow and made sure he lent money to those businesses. Europeans trusted Morgan's judgment and gave him money to invest. He used it to build American businesses. The investors received profits.

Morgan became the primary financier (fih-nan-SUHR) for large companies, which means that he loaned these companies lots of money. At the height of his career, he controlled banks, railroads, insurance companies, and shipping lines. In fact, he was so powerful that some people worried that he wanted to take control of the entire country.

The Assembly Line Is Born

Henry Ford was born in Michigan in 1863. At age 16, Ford walked to Detroit to take a job at a machine shop. Later, he went to work for a large shipbuilder. After learning all about motors, Ford and two partners formed Ford Motor Company in 1903 to build automobiles. At first, these automobiles cost so much that only the wealthy could purchase them. In 1908, Ford introduced the Model T, which was very popular and less expensive than prior automobiles. More than 10,000 were sold the first year, and Ford Motor Company could not keep up with the customer demand.

Then, Ford invented the assembly line. Men stood along a conveyor (kuhn-VAY-uhr) belt. As an engine moved past, each worker did one job, which sped up the process. As the cost to make an automobile fell, Ford dropped the selling price, and more people could afford a car. The era of the automobile had arrived.

Comprehension Question

Describe at least two things that made J. P. Morgan a success.

© Shell Education

European Immigration

Some people in Europe were living in crowded cities. They were hungry and poor. They could not find jobs. Some people had trouble because of their religions. Wars took lives and land. This was the case in Europe in the late 1800s and early 1900s. So, millions of people left Europe in the late 1800s and early 1900s. They migrated, or moved, to the United States. Many people sold all they owned and bought ship tickets.

An immigrant (IM-muh-gruhnt) is a person who moves to a new land. About 27 million immigrants came to America between 1870 and 1916. Each one hoped to have a better life. Some of them did. Others did not.

Entering Ellis Island

The immigrants came on ships. They went to Ellis Island. Ellis Island is in New York Harbor. People went into the station. They had to pass health tests. Doctors said no to some of them. Those who were ill or insane could not stay. Neither could those who had spent time in jail.

About two percent (2%) of the people were excluded (ek-SKLOOD-uhd). This meant that they could not stay. They had to get on ships. They had to go back. If it was a child, one parent had to go, too. So, some families split up. They sometimes never saw one another again.

Abusing Immigrant Workers

Starting a new life was hard. Most immigrants lived in tenements (TEN-uh-muhnts). These were run-down buildings. They lacked fresh air and sunlight. Landlords owned them. They charged rent. Up to 32 families were crammed into one building.

Finding work was easy. But the pay was poor. The working conditions were bad. Factory owners set up sweatshops. These buildings had no windows. Workers could not speak. They could not use the bathroom. The workers did not get breaks. Most of the workers were women and children. They needed the jobs. If they did not work, they had no money. Then they could not eat.

37

Sweatshop owners exploited (eks-PLOIT-uhd) immigrants. They treated them badly. They paid male immigrants less than other workers. Females got even less. Needlework and cigar-making companies hired lots of immigrants.

Some families worked in their apartments. Even small children worked. They did piecework for pennies. Piecework was stitching seams. It was sewing small things together. The people were paid for each piece. They worked all the time. They worked seven days a week. Yet, they made just enough money to live.

The Working Child

Lots of immigrant children worked in bad places. They worked in sweatshops, coal mines, and textile (TEKS-tile) mills. They had no time for school. So, they had no hope of getting out of these places.

Textile mills made cloth. Knitting machines and cloth looms were not safe. Yet, children worked these machines. If they got sleepy or could not move fast enough, they were hurt or killed. But the textile mill owners did not care! There were lots of other children to take their places.

Then, Lewis Hine took photos. He sent them to newspapers. His photos showed children in bad conditions and awful places. People were shocked. They urged leaders to end child labor.

A Mix of Cultures

America is a mix of cultures. No place else on Earth has had so many immigrants. They brought their ideas with them. Each group added to the country in its own way.

Comprehension Question

Why did some people leave their homelands?

#50084 — *Leveled Texts: The 20th Century*

© *Shell Education*

European Immigration

Picture living in a crowded country. You are hungry. You are poor. There are lots of other poor people, too. They cannot find jobs. Some people are harassed (huh-RASD), or in trouble, due to their religions. Wars took lives and land. This was the case in Europe in the late 1800s and early 1900s. So, millions of people left. They migrated, or moved, to the United States. Many people sold all they owned and bought ship tickets.

An immigrant (IM-muh-gruhnt) is a person who moves to a new land. About 27 million immigrants came to America between 1870 and 1916. These people hoped they would have better lives. Some people did. Others did not.

Entering Ellis Island

Immigrants came on ships. They went to Ellis Island. Ellis Island is in New York Harbor. People went into the station. They had to pass health tests. Inspectors rejected some people. Any person who was ill, insane, or had spent time in jail could not enter the country.

About two percent (2%) of the people were excluded (ek-SKLOOD-uhd). This meant that they could not stay. They had to get on ships. They had to go back home. If a child was excluded, at least one parent had to go, too. In this way, some families were split up. They sometimes never saw one another again.

Abusing Immigrant Workers

Starting a new life was hard. Most immigrants lived in tenements (TEN-uh-muhnts). Tenements were run-down buildings that lacked fresh air and sunlight. Greedy landlords owned them. They charged rent. Up to 32 families were crammed into one building. About 4,000 immigrants lived on each city block.

Finding work was easy. But, the pay was very bad and the conditions were awful. Factory owners set up sweatshops. These buildings were dark. They had no windows. Workers could not speak or use the bathroom. They were not given breaks. Most of the workers were women and children. They did not complain. If they did not work, they had no money. Then, they could not eat.

(39)

Many immigrants came without a cent. The sweatshop owners exploited (eks-PLOIT-uhd) them. This means they were not fair to them. They paid male immigrants less than other workers. Female immigrants earned even less. Needlework and cigar-making companies hired a lot of immigrants.

Some families worked in their apartments. Even the children worked. They did piecework for pennies. Piecework included sewing seams or stitching small items together. The immigrants were paid for each piece they did. They worked all the time. Yet, they barely made enough money to live.

The Working Child

Many immigrant children worked in bad conditions. They had no time for school. So, they had no hope of getting out of the sweatshops, coal mines, and textile (TEKS-tile) mills.

Textile mill owners mistreated their workers. Knitting machines and cloth looms were not safe. Yet, children worked these machines. If they got sleepy or could not move fast enough, they were hurt or even killed. But, the mill owners did not care! There were lots of other children to take their places.

Then, Lewis Hine took photos. He sent them to newspapers. His photos showed children working in bad conditions and awful places. People were shocked. They urged the nation's leaders to end child labor.

A Mix of Cultures

America is a mix of cultures. No place else on Earth has had so many immigrants. Newcomers brought their ideas with them. Each group added to the country in its own way.

Comprehension Question

What made immigrants want to come to the United States?

#50084— *Leveled Texts: The 20th Century*

© Shell Education

European Immigration

Imagine living in an overcrowded country with many other poor, desperate people who cannot find jobs. Some people are harassed (huh-RASD) because of their religions. Wars are ruining lives and land. This was the scene in Europe during the late nineteenth and early twentieth centuries. So, millions of people left. They migrated to the United States. Many people sold all they owned to buy ship tickets.

About 27 million immigrants (IM-muh-gruhntz) arrived in America between 1870 and 1916. Most came from Europe. These people thought that they would have better lives. This was not always the case.

Entering Ellis Island

Immigrants came on ships to Ellis Island. It's near the Statue of Liberty in New York Harbor. There, people had to pass medical and oral tests. Inspectors rejected those who were ill, insane, or had spent time in prison. Most people spent about four hours in the station.

About two percent of the people were excluded (ek-SKLOOD-uhd). This meant that they could not enter the country. They had to get on ships and go back where they came from. If a child was excluded, at least one parent had to leave, too. In this way, some families were split up. They sometimes never saw one another again.

Abusing Immigrant Workers

Starting a new life was hard. Most immigrants lived in tenements (TEN-uh-muhnts). Greedy landlords owned these run-down buildings that lacked fresh air and sunlight. Up to 32 families were crammed into one building. About 4,000 immigrants lived on each city block.

Finding work was easy. But, the pay was poor and the working conditions were horrible. Factory owners set up sweatshops. These dimly lit buildings had no windows. Sometimes, workers could not speak or use the bathroom. They were not given breaks. Most of the workers were women and children. They did not dare to complain. If they did not work, they had no money. They would go hungry.

41

Many immigrants arrived without a cent. The sweatshop owners exploited (eks-PLOIT-uhd) them. Business owners paid male immigrants less than other workers. Female immigrants earned even less. The needlework and cigar-making industries hired a lot of immigrants.

Outside of the sweatshops, whole families worked in their apartments. They did piecework for pennies. Piecework included sewing seams or stitching small items together. The immigrants were paid for every piece they completed. They barely made enough to get by.

The Working Child

Many immigrant children worked in bad conditions. Some children were injured or killed on the job. And since they had no time for school, they had no hope of escaping the sweatshops, coal mines, and textile (TEKS-tile) mills.

Textile mill owners treated their workers badly. Knitting machines and fabric looms were unsafe. Yet, children often worked these machines. Those children who grew sleepy or could not move fast enough got hurt or killed. But, the mill owners did not care! There were other children to take their places.

Then, Lewis Hine sent photos to newspapers. His photos showed children working in terrible conditions and awful places. When people saw them, they urged the government to end child labor.

A Mix of Cultures

America is a mix of many cultures. No place else on Earth has had so many immigrants. Newcomers brought their ideas with them. Each group added to the country in its own way.

Comprehension Question

Describe at least three reasons immigrants came to the United States.

#50084—Leveled Texts: The 20th Century

© Shell Education

European Immigration

Imagine living in an overcrowded country with other poor, desperate people and few jobs. Some people are harassed (huh-RASD) because of their religious beliefs. Wars are destroying lives and land. This was the scene in Europe during the late nineteenth and early twentieth centuries. So, millions of people migrated to the United States. Many people sold all they owned to buy ship tickets, which made their decisions irrevocable (ir-REH-vuh-kuh-buhl).

About 27 million immigrants (IM-muh-gruhntz) arrived in America between 1870 and 1916. Most were Europeans. These people thought that they would have better lives, but this was not always true.

Entering Ellis Island

European immigrants came via ships to Ellis Island near the Statue of Liberty in New York Harbor. Inside the station, people had to pass medical and oral tests. Inspectors rejected all those who were ill, insane, or had spent time in prison. Most people spent about four hours in the station.

About two percent of the people were excluded (ek-SKLOOD-uhd), which meant that they could not enter the country. They had to get on ships and return to their home countries. If a child was excluded, at least one parent had to leave, too. Exclusion caused some families to split up and never see one another again.

Abusing Immigrant Workers

Starting a new life was difficult. Most immigrants lived in tenements (TEN-uh-muhnts). Greedy landlords owned these run-down firetraps that lacked fresh air and sunlight. Up to 32 families were crammed into each building. About 4,000 immigrants lived on each city block.

Finding work was easy, but the pay was poor and the working conditions horrible. Factory owners set up sweatshops in dimly lit buildings with no windows. Sometimes, workers could not speak or use the bathroom. There was no such thing as a break. Most of the workers were women and children who did not dare to complain. They knew that if they did not work, they would have no money to purchase food.

43

Many immigrants arrived penniless and were exploited (eks-PLOIT-uhd) by the sweatshop owners. Business owners paid male immigrants less than other workers, and female immigrants earned even less. The needlework and cigar-making industries used immigrant laborers.

Outside of the sweatshops, entire families worked in their one-room apartments. They did piecework for pennies. Piecework included sewing seams or stitching small items together. The immigrants were paid for every piece they completed. The family barely made a living.

The Working Child

Many immigrant children worked in such bad conditions that some children were injured or even killed on the job. And since they had no time for school, they had no hope of escaping the sweatshops, coal mines, and textile (TEKS-tile) mills.

Textile mill owners treated their workers badly. Knitting machines and fabric looms were dangerous, yet children often operated these machines. Those children who grew sleepy or could not move fast enough got hurt. But, the mill owners did not care! They knew there were other children to take the places of those who were injured or killed.

Then, Lewis Hine sent photos to newspapers. His photos showed children working in terrible conditions and awful places. When people saw them, they urged the government to end child labor.

A Mix of Cultures

America is a mix of many cultures. No place else on Earth has had so many immigrants. Newcomers brought their ideas with them, and each group added to the country in its own way.

Comprehension Question

For what reasons were the steps of becoming a U.S. citizen worth it for immigrants in the early 1900s?

#50084—Leveled Texts: The 20th Century

© Shell Education

Asian Immigration

About 200 years ago, a lot of people in China were poor. Some people had no food. In 1850, they heard news. Gold had been found in California. Chinese men risked their lives to go to California. They heard that the U.S. railroads and mines had jobs, too. More men left. The Chinese ruler did not want them to go. So, they had to sneak onto ships. If caught, the Chinese men would die. But, they felt it was worth the risk. They wanted new lives.

It was hard to come to the United States as an immigrant (IM-muh-gruhnt). An immigrant is a person who moves to a new land. The people had to learn English. Asians looked different from most Americans. Many Chinese people kept their traditions and clothing. They were attacked for how they spoke, looked, and dressed. The Chinese felt safer in groups. So, they lived near one another in cities. They formed Chinatowns.

Racism Rears its Ugly Head

Asians were paid less than other workers. Some people would not hire them. So, Chinese people opened businesses. They ran places to eat. They washed clothes. They had stores. They worked hard. Yet, many people really disliked them. In 1882, Congress passed a law. It was the Chinese Exclusion (ek-SKLOO-shuhn) Act. Exclusion means to keep out. After that, just a few Chinese people could come to America.

Then, in 1906, there was an earthquake. It caused a big fire. The fire was in San Francisco, California. Important papers burned. This left no way to show who was a U.S. citizen. Many men from China lived in the city at the time. They wanted to be U.S. citizens. So, they said they were born in the United States. This made them U.S. citizens. And, their children were U.S. citizens, too. The men wrote to their families. They told them to come to America.

Angel Island Was Not Heaven

Many of the Chinese men's families came. To stop them, the Angel Island Immigration Station opened in 1910. It was in the San Francisco Bay. Workers kept all Chinese people in a building there. It was hot and dirty. Guards locked them in small cells. The cells looked like zoo cages. The people were rarely let out. Guards threw food on the cell floors. Some people lived like this for months.

© Shell Education   #50084— Leveled Texts: The 20th Century

The people had to answer questions. They were asked about their towns and homes. They were asked about all their family members. The people had to prove they had family members who were American citizens. The U.S. citizens had to answer the same questions. The answers from both had to be the same. If not, inspectors rejected the new immigrants. About one in ten were excluded (ek-SKLOOD-uhd). This meant they could not stay. They had to go back to China.

Just a Few Allowed

A quota (KWOH-tuh) is a number. In 1921, Congress made quotas. It set how many people could come to the United States each year. Some places, like England and France, could send a lot. But few Asians were let in. Then, the National Origins Act passed in 1924. It set new quotas. This act meant even fewer Asians could come.

In World War II, U.S. troops went overseas. While away, some soldiers got married. The War Brides Act let them bring their wives and children to America. In 1952, the Immigration and Nationality (nash-uh-NAL-uh-tee) Act set new quotas. It let in more Asians. Asians could become U.S. citizens. It had taken a hundred years. But at last, the Asians were on their way to equality.

Comprehension Question

Why did Angel Island Immigration Station open in 1910? What was it like there?

#50084— Leveled Texts: The 20th Century
© Shell Education

Asian Immigration

A lot of people in China were poor in the 1800s. Some people were starving. In 1850, they heard news. It was about the gold rush in California. Chinese men risked their lives to go there. Then, they heard that the U.S. railroads and mines needed workers, too. More men left. The Chinese ruler did not want the men to go. So, they had to sneak onto ships. If caught, they faced death. But, they thought it was worth the risk. They wanted better lives.

Coming to the United States was tough. Immigrants (IM-muh-gruhntz) had to learn English on their own. The Asians had a really hard time since they looked different from most Americans. Many Chinese people kept their traditions and clothing. They were attacked for how they spoke, looked, and dressed. For comfort, they gathered in cities. That's how Chinatowns formed.

Racism Rears its Ugly Head

Asians earned less than others doing the same work. Some people would not hire them. So, they opened their own businesses. They ran stores and laundries. They had restaurants. They worked hard. Yet, many people really disliked them. In 1882, Congress cut back on Chinese immigration. It passed the Chinese Exclusion (ek-SKLOO-shuhn) Act. Exclusion means to keep out. The act said that just a few Chinese people could come into the country each year.

Then, in April 1906, there was an earthquake and fire in San Francisco, California. It ruined many legal records. There was no way to prove who was a U.S. citizen. Many Chinese men lived in the city at the time. They saw this as their chance to be U.S. citizens. They said they were born in the United States. This made them and their children U.S. citizens. The men told their families to come to America.

Angel Island Was Not Heaven

To stop the Chinese from coming, the Angel Island Immigration Station opened in 1910. It was in the San Francisco Bay. The workers kept all Chinese people in a building there. The place was hot and dirty. Guards locked people in small, smelly cells. The cells looked like zoo cages. The people were rarely let out. Guards threw their food on the cell floors. Some people lived in these awful conditions for months.

Immigrants had to answer questions. They were asked about their towns, home lives, and family. The people had to prove that they had family members who were American citizens. The U.S. citizens had to answer the same questions. If the answers from both were not the same, the inspectors rejected the new immigrants. About 10 percent of all the immigrants were excluded (ek-SKLOOD-uhd). This meant they could not stay.

Just a Few Allowed

In 1921, Congress made quotas (KWOH-tuhz). The quotas set the number of people who could move to the United States each year. Some nations, like England and France, could send a lot of people. But few Asians were allowed. When the National Origins Act went into effect in 1924, it set new quotas. After that, even fewer Asians could come to the United States.

Then, World War II took U.S. soldiers overseas to fight. While away, some soldiers got married. The War Brides Act let them bring their wives and children to America. In 1952, the Immigration and Nationality (nash-uh-NAL-uh-tee) Act set new quotas. This act finally let in more people from Asia. U.S. citizenship was offered to Asian immigrants. It had taken a hundred years. But at last, the Asians were on the road to equality.

Comprehension Question

Describe the Angel Island Immigration Station.

© Shell Education

Asian Immigration

In the 1800s, many people in China were poor and starving. In 1850, they heard about the gold rush in California. Chinese men risked their lives to go there. More men left when they heard that the U.S. railroads and mines needed laborers. The Chinese emperor would not let the men leave the country. So, they had to sneak onto ships. If caught, they faced death. But, they were desperate for a better life.

Coming to the United States was hard. Immigrants (IM-muh-gruhntz) had to learn English without training. The Asians had an especially hard time because they looked different from the majority of Americans. Many of them kept their traditions and clothing. They were attacked for how they spoke, looked, and dressed. So, for comfort, they clustered in neighborhoods. That's how Chinatowns formed in cities.

Racism Rears its Ugly Head

Some people would not hire Asian immigrants, and those who did, paid them less than other workers. But the immigrants were smart and resourceful. They opened their own businesses. They had restaurants, stores, and laundries. Still, no matter how hard they worked, many people were against them. In 1882, Congress reduced Chinese immigration. It passed the Chinese Exclusion (ek-SKLOO-shuhn) Act. After that, just a small number of Chinese people could come into the country each year.

Then, in April 1906, an earthquake and fire ruined all legal records in San Francisco, California. This left no way to prove who was a U.S. citizen. Many Chinese men living there jumped at this chance. They claimed they were born in the United States. This made them and their children American citizens. The men urged their families to rush to America.

Angel Island Was Not Heaven

To stop the Chinese from coming, the Angel Island Immigration Station opened in 1910. It was in the San Francisco Bay. There, the officials detained all Chinese people. The buildings were hot and dirty. Guards locked people in small, smelly cells. The cells looked like zoo cages. The people were rarely let outside. Guards threw food on the floor for them to eat. Some people lived in these awful conditions for months.

© Shell Education #50084— Leveled Texts: The 20th Century

Each immigrant faced a Board of Special Inquiry. The board asked questions about the person's home life, family background, and village. The immigrants had to prove that they had family members who were American citizens. The U.S. citizens then had to answer the questions, too. If the answers from both people were not the same, the inspectors rejected the new immigrants. About 10 percent of all the immigrants were excluded (ek-SKLOOD-uhd). This meant they could not stay.

Just a Few Allowed

In 1921, Congress set quotas (KWOH-tuhz). These quotas set the number of people who could move to the United States each year. Some nations, like England and France, could send a lot of people. But, few Asians were allowed. When the National Origins Act went into effect in 1924, it set new quotas. After that, even fewer Asians could immigrate to the United States.

Then, World War II took many U.S. soldiers overseas to fight. While away, some soldiers married. The War Brides Act let them bring their spouses and children to America. In 1952, the Immigration and Nationality (nash-uh-NAL-uh-tee) Act set new quotas. This act finally let in people from Asia. U.S. citizenship was finally offered to Asian immigrants. It had taken a hundred years. But at last, the Asians were on the road to equality.

Comprehension Question

Describe at least three aspects of the experience at Angel Island for Asian immigrants.

© Shell Education

Asian Immigration

In the 1800s, in China, many people were impoverished and starving. In 1850, they heard about the gold rush in California. Chinese men risked their lives to go to America. More men left when they heard that the U.S. railroads and mines needed laborers. The Chinese emperor refused to allow the men leave the country. So, they had to sneak aboard ships. If caught, they faced the death penalty. But, they were desperate for a better life.

Coming to the United States was difficult. All immigrants (IM-muh-gruhntz) had to learn English without training. The Asians had an especially tough time because they looked different from the majority of Americans. Chinese immigrants who kept their traditions and clothing were attacked for how they spoke, looked, or dressed. So, for comfort, they clustered in neighborhoods, which is how Chinatowns formed in cities.

Racism Rears its Ugly Head

Some people would not hire Asian immigrants, and those who did, paid them less than other workers. So, these smart and resourceful immigrants opened their own businesses. They operated restaurants, stores, and laundries. Yet, no matter how hard they worked, many people were against them. In 1882, Congress reduced Chinese immigration with the Chinese Exclusion (ek-SKLOO-shuhn) Act. After that, only a small number of Chinese people could immigrate to the United States each year.

Then, in April 1906, an earthquake and fire destroyed all legal records in San Francisco, California, leaving no way to prove who was a United States citizen. Many Chinese men living in the area jumped at this chance and claimed they were born in the United States. This made them and their children American citizens. The men urged their families to rush to America.

Angel Island Was Not Heaven

To stop the Chinese influx (IN-fluhkz), the Angel Island Immigration Station opened in 1910 in the San Francisco Bay. Officials detained all Asians there in hot, filthy buildings. Guards locked people in small, smelly cells that looked like zoo cages. The people were rarely allowed outdoors. Guards threw small amounts of food on the floor for them to eat. Some people lived in these terrible conditions for months.

51

The Board of Special Inquiry asked each immigrant questions about the person's home life, family background, and village. The immigrants had to prove that they had relatives who were American citizens. The U.S. citizens had to answer identical questions. If the answers from both people were not the same, the inspectors rejected the newcomers. About 10 percent of all the immigrants were excluded (ek-SKLOOD-uhd) and forced to leave the country.

Just a Few Allowed

In 1921, Congress set quotas (KWOH-tuhz) to limit the number of people who could immigrate to the United States each year. European nations could send many people, but few Asians were allowed. When the National Origins Act went into effect in 1924, it set even lower quotas. Then, even fewer Asians could immigrate.

During World War II, many U.S. soldiers fought overseas. While away, some of the soldiers got married. The War Brides Act let them bring their spouses and children into the country. In 1952, the Immigration and Nationality (nash-uh-NAL-uh-tee) Act set new quotas that finally allowed more Asians, and citizenship was offered to many Asian immigrants. It had taken a hundred years to put the Asians on the road to equality.

Comprehension Question

In what ways did the experience at Angel Island go against the American ideals of life, liberty, and the pursuit of happiness?

© *Shell Education*

World War I: The "Great War"

A war began in 1914. It took place in Europe. More nations fought in this "Great War" than in any war before. The war lasted for four years. About 65 million men fought. More than 19 million people died. It is one of the worst human disasters of all time. Today, we call it World War I.

The War Begins

Archduke Francis Ferdinand was going to be a king. He would rule Austria-Hungary (AW-stree-uh HUHNG-guh-ree). He and his wife went to Bosnia (BAHZ-nee-uh). A man assassinated (uh-SAS-uh-nay-tuhd) them. This means he killed them. The man who shot them lived in Serbia (SIR-be-uh). So, Austria-Hungary blamed Serbia for the deaths. Austria-Hungary declared war on Serbia. Soon, other countries joined in. The Germans declared war on France. Great Britain wanted to stop Germany. So, Great Britain entered the war.

By August 1914, there were two alliances (uh-LYE-uhntz-ez), or groups, and they were enemies. Austria-Hungary and Germany were the Central Powers. The Allies were Great Britain, France, and Russia. The Central Powers were against the Allies.

The War Grows

German troops came on strong. They attacked Serbia. They drove the Russians out of Poland. They pushed them from the states that border Russia. The Germans felt things were going well. They planned to build an empire. An empire is a group of nations that has the same ruler.

Germany wanted to stop ships. Ships carried munitions (myoo-NIH-shunz). Munitions are guns, bullets, and bombs. So in February 1915, Germany said that Great Britain's waters were a war zone. Germany said it would sink all boats. It would tell its submarines to sink every ship.

53

This threat included U.S. ships. U.S. President Woodrow Wilson did not want to take sides. But the threats made him mad. So, Germany backed down. Germany did not want to bring the United States into the war. Then, in January 1917, Germany fired on all ships, including U.S. ships. The German leader said this would win the war. Ships sank. Some U.S. citizens died. President Wilson stopped talking to Germany.

A Famous Telegram

In early 1917, a British spy intercepted (in-tur-SEP-tuhd) a secret note. This means he got one of the enemy's messages. The spy secretly read the message. A German had written it. His name was Arthur Zimmermann. So, the telegram is called the Zimmermann telegram. In the telegram, Germany asked Mexico to join sides with them. It said that Germany would own the United States after the war. Then, Germany would give Mexico land from the United States.

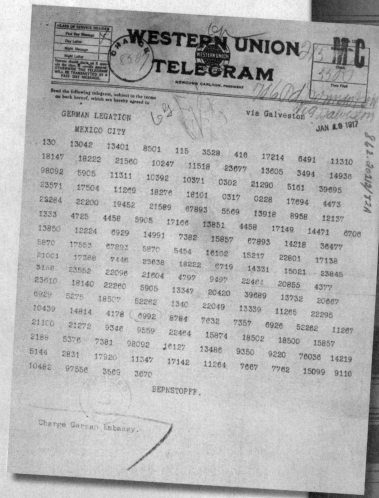

The American people heard about this. They were mad. The United States joined the Allies. This was bad news for the Central Powers. They would lose the war.

The Central Powers Weaken

By November 1918, Germany asked for peace talks. On November 11, 1918, Germany signed an armistice (ARE-muhs-tuhs), or peace treaty. The Allies won the war. So, they set the terms. Germany had to give up its air force. It had to give up its navy. It could keep an army of just 100,000 men.

The war had cost the Allies a lot of money. They told Germany to pay them back. But this was a big burden. It ruined the German economy. It set the stage for another world war.

Comprehension Question

What did the Zimmermann telegram promise Mexico?

#50084— *Leveled Texts: The 20th Century*

© Shell Education

World War I: The "Great War"

In 1914, a war began. At that time, it was called the "Great War." It was fought in Europe. More nations battled in it than in any war before it. It lasted for four years. About 65 million troops fought. More than 19 million people died. It is one of the worst human disasters of all time. Now we call it World War I.

The War Begins

Archduke Francis Ferdinand was going to be a king. He would rule Austria-Hungary (AW-stree-uh HUHNG-guh-ree). He and his wife visited Bosnia (BAHZ-nee-uh). A Bosnian (BAHZ-nee-uhn) assassinated (uh-SAS-uh-nay-tuhd) them. This means he killed them. The man lived in Serbia (SIR-be-uh). So, Austria-Hungary blamed Serbia for the deaths. It declared war on Serbia. Soon, other nations in Europe joined in. The Germans declared war on France. Great Britain wanted to stop Germany. So, it entered the war.

By the middle of August 1914, there were two sides fighting the war. This means that there were two alliances (uh-LYE-uhntz-ez), or groups. Austria-Hungary and Germany were the Central Powers. The Allies were Great Britain, France, and Russia. The Central Powers and the Allies fought each other. They were enemies.

The War Grows

At first, it seemed like Germany would win. German troops attacked Serbia. They pushed the Russians out of Poland. They pushed them out of the states that border Russia. The Germans planned to have a huge empire. An empire is a group of nations that has the same ruler.

U.S. President Woodrow Wilson did not want to take sides. In February 1915, Germany said that the waters around Great Britain were a war zone. It wanted to stop ships that carried munitions (myoo-NIH-shunz) to the Allies. Munitions are guns, bullets, and bombs. The Germans said that they would wreck all boats. Their submarines would sink every ship.

This included U.S. ships, too. It made President Wilson mad. So, Germany backed down from its threat. The Germans did not want to bring the United States into the war. But then, in January 1917, Germany changed its mind. It fired on all ships. The German leaders said this would win the war. Ships sank. Some U.S. citizens died. President Wilson broke off talks with Germany.

A Famous Telegram

In early 1917, the British intercepted (in-tur-SEP-tuhd) a secret message. This means they secretly got an enemy message. Then, they read it. A German leader named Arthur Zimmermann had written it. In the Zimmermann telegram, Germany asked Mexico to join them. It said that Germany would own the United States after the war. Then, it would give Mexico land from the United States. The American people heard about Germany's plan. They were mad. The United States joined the Allies. This was bad news for the Central Powers.

The Central Powers Weaken

By November 1918, Germany asked for peace talks. On November 11, 1918, Germany signed an armistice (ARE-muhs-tuhs). An armistice is a peace treaty. Since the Allies won the war, they decided the terms. Germany had to give up its air force and its navy. It could keep a standing army of just 100,000 men.

The war had cost the Allies a lot. They wanted Germany to pay them back. This was a big burden. It ruined the German economy. And, it set the stage for another big world war.

Comprehension Question

What was the Zimmermann telegram about?

#50084—Leveled Texts: The 20th Century

© Shell Education

World War I: The "Great War"

In 1914, the "Great War" began in Europe. More nations battled in this war than in any war before it. It lasted for four years. A total of 65 million soldiers fought. More than 19 million people died. It is one of the worst human disasters ever. Today, we call it World War I.

The War Begins

Archduke Francis Ferdinand was the future king of Austria-Hungary (AW-stree-uh HUHNG-guh-ree). He and his wife traveled to Bosnia (BAHZ-nee-uh). While there, a Bosnian (BAHZ-nee-uhn) man assassinated (uh-SAS-uh-nay-tuhd) them. The killer lived in Serbia (SIR-be-uh). So, Austria-Hungary leaders blamed Serbia for the murders. They declared war on Serbia. Soon, some of the powerful nations in Europe joined the war. The Germans declared war on France. Great Britain wanted to stop Germany and entered the war.

By the middle of August 1914, the two sides were clear. There were two great alliances (uh-LYE-uhntz-ez). Austria-Hungary and Germany were the Central Powers. On the other side were the Allies of Great Britain, France, and Russia.

The War Grows

At first, it seemed like Germany was unstoppable. German troops attacked Serbia. They pushed the Russians out of Poland and the Baltic States (Estonia, Lithuania, and Latvia). These states bordered Russia. Things were going so well that the Germans began to plan a huge German empire in eastern Europe.

U.S. President Woodrow Wilson did not want to take sides in Europe's war. In February 1915, Germany said that the waters around Great Britain were a war zone. It wanted to stop the ships that carried munitions (myoo-NIH-shunz) to Great Britain. Munitions were guns, bullets, and bombs. The Germans said that its submarines would torpedo all boats in those waters.

57

© Shell Education

This included U.S. ships, too. It made President Wilson angry. Germany backed down from its threat. It did not want to bring America into the war. But then, in January 1917, Germany changed its mind. It fired on all ships. The German leaders thought it was the only way to win the war. When ships sank, some U.S. citizens died. President Wilson broke off talks with Germany.

A Famous Telegram

In early 1917, the United States learned shocking information. The British intercepted (in-tur-SEP-tuhd) a message to Mexico. A German official named Arthur Zimmermann had written the telegram. In the Zimmermann telegram, Germany asked Mexico to join the Central Powers. The Germans said they would own the United States after the war and would give Mexico land from the United States. When the American people found out about Germany's plan, they were upset. The United States joined the Allies. It was the beginning of the end for the Central Powers.

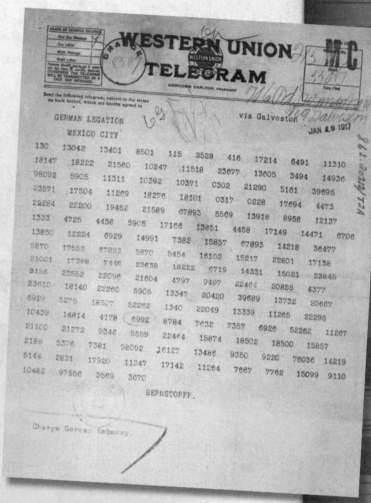

The Central Powers Weaken

By November 1918, Germany had asked for peace talks with the Allies. On November 11, 1918, Germany signed an armistice (ARE-muhs-tuhs). The Allies decided the terms of this peace treaty since they had won the war. Germany had to give up its air force and its navy and could only maintain a standing army of 100,000 men.

The war had cost the Allies a lot of money. They expected Germany to pay them back. This was a heavy burden, and the Germans complained. However, the Allies made the Germans accept all the blame for the war. This ruined the German economy and set the stage for World War II.

Comprehension Question

Why did the Zimmermann telegram upset the American people?

58

© Shell Education

World War I: The "Great War"

In 1914, the "Great War" began in Europe and lasted for four years. More countries battled in this war than in any war before it. A total of 65 million soldiers fought and more than 19 million people perished in one of the worst human disasters in history. Today, we call this conflict World War I.

The War Begins

Archduke Francis Ferdinand was the future king of Austria-Hungary (AW-stree-uh HUHNG-guh-ree). He and his wife, Sophie, traveled to Bosnia (BAHZ-nee-uh). While there, a Bosnian (BAHZ-nee-uhn) man assassinated (uh-SAS-uh-nay-tuhd) them. The killer lived in Serbia (SIR-be-uh). So, Austria-Hungary's leaders blamed Serbia for their murders and declared war on Serbia. Soon, some of the powerful nations in Europe joined the conflict. The Germans declared war on France, and Great Britain wanted to stop Germany. The British entered the war.

By the middle of August 1914, two major alliances (uh-LYE-uhntz-ez) had formed. On one side of the conflict were the Central Powers of Austria-Hungary and Germany. Opposing them were the Allies, consisting of Great Britain, France, and Russia.

The War Grows

Initially, it seemed like the German army was undefeatable. German troops attacked Serbia and pushed the Russians out of Poland. They defeated the Russians in the Baltic States (Estonia, Lithuania, and Latvia) on the coast of the Baltic Sea. These states also bordered Russia. Things were going so well that the Germans began planning a huge German empire in eastern Europe.

U.S. President Woodrow Wilson refused to take sides in Europe's war. In February 1915, Germany announced that the waters around Great Britain were a war zone.

© Shell Education   #50084—Leveled Texts: The 20th Century

The Germans declared that they would torpedo all ships in those waters in order to stop munitions (myoo-NIH-shunz) (guns, ammunition, and bombs) from reaching Great Britain.

This included U.S. ships and made President Wilson so angry that Germany backed down from its threat. The Germans did not want to bring America into the war. But in January 1917, Germany started firing on all ships because its leaders thought it was the only way to win. Many ships went down, and some American citizens died. President Wilson broke off official talks with Germany.

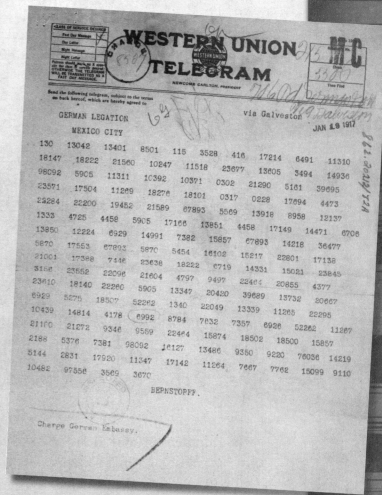

A Famous Telegram

In early 1917, the United States learned shocking information. The British had intercepted (in-tur-SEP-tuhd) a coded telegram to Mexico. A German official named Arthur Zimmermann wrote the telegram. In the Zimmermann telegram, Germany encouraged Mexico to join the Central Powers. The Germans said they would control the United States after the war and would give Mexico land from the United States. When the American people discovered Germany's plan, they were furious, and the United States entered World War I on the side of the Allies. It was the beginning of the end for the Central Powers.

The Central Powers Weaken

By November 1918, Germany had requested peace talks with the Allies. On November 11, 1918, Germany signed an armistice (ARE-muhs-tuhs). Since they won, the Allies established the terms of this peace treaty. Germany had to give up its air force and its navy and could only maintain a standing army of 100,000 men.

The war had been expensive for the Allies, and they expected Germany to pay them back. Unfortunately, this heavy burden ruined the German economy and set the stage for World War II.

Comprehension Question

How did the Zimmermann telegram affect Wilson's decision to join the war?

#50084—Leveled Texts: The 20th Century

© Shell Education

The Roaring Twenties

World War I ended in 1918. Then, the way Americans lived changed. Many people were doing well. Some of them were rich. People bought new clothes. They tried new dances. They ate, drank, and had fun. This time was called the Roaring Twenties.

During the Great War, the men left. They had to go fight. So, women did the men's jobs. Some people had said that women were not as good as men. They said that women were not as smart or as strong. The women proved them wrong.

Women wanted to vote. Suffragists (SUHF-rih-jists) worked for the right to vote. Women had tried to get the right to vote for a long time. In 1920, their dreams came true. A law passed. It said that women could vote. It was the Nineteenth Amendment. It was added to the U.S. Constitution (kon-stuh-TOO-shuhn). All women age 21 or older could vote.

The Harlem Renaissance

African Americans had a hard time in the early 1900s. They did not have the same rights as whites. They could not drink at a "Whites Only" water fountain. They had to find a "Colored" fountain. In stores, they had to use different doors. They could not go to the same schools, either. They had to sit in the backs of buses. This was segregation (seg-ruh-GAY-shuhn). It was due to their skin color. It was wrong.

A group formed in 1909. This group stood up for the rights of African Americans. It was the National Association for the Advancement of Colored People (NAACP). The NAACP wanted people to know how African Americans were mistreated. This group is still active today.

In the 1920s, the Great Migration (my-GRAY-shuhn) took place. Migration means people moved to new places. Many African Americans left the South. They wanted better lives. They moved to the North and the West. They went to cities. There, they got jobs.

Harlem is in New York City. A renaissance (reh-nuh-SAWNTS) occurred there. A renaissance is a time of great growth and change. African American writers, singers, and poets lived in Harlem. They wrote and sang about their lives. They touched the hearts of others. A lot of Harlem Renaissance artists are still famous. Louis Armstrong played the trumpet. Bessie Smith sang. Duke Ellington played jazz. Some people say this was the start of the Civil Rights Movement.

A Dark Day in History

Many things changed during the first 30 years of the 1900s. Women worked outside of their homes. African Americans had success in the arts. Banks loaned cash. Many people had cars. The mood of the nation was good.

But that changed on October 29, 1929. On Black Tuesday, the stock market crashed. This means that the stocks they had bought were worth much less than they had paid for them. People had borrowed money to buy the stocks. Now, those stocks were worth very little. But, people still owed

money to the banks. The bankers wanted their money plus interest. Interest is extra money paid when people borrow money. Most people did not have the cash. They could not pay back the banks.

People went to the banks. They tried to take out their cash. But borrowers did not pay back their loans because they did not have any money. So, the banks had no cash, either. The banks closed! People lost all their savings. Companies shut down. People lost their jobs. They could not pay for their houses. So, they lost their homes, too. They slept under bridges. Lots of people were hungry. This was the start of the Great Depression (dih-PRESH-uhn). It was a sad, hard time.

Comprehension Question

What did some people think about women before World War I?

#50084— Leveled Texts: The 20th Century

© Shell Education

The Roaring Twenties

World War I ended in 1918. After the war, the way people lived in the United States changed. Many Americans were doing well. Some of them were rich. People tried new ways of dancing and dressing. They ate, drank, and had fun. This time was called the Roaring Twenties.

During the Great War, men left. They went to fight. So, women did the men's jobs. Before that time, some people did not think that women were equal to men. They said that women were not as smart or as strong. Women proved them wrong. They had done the men's jobs.

Women wanted to be able to vote. Women suffragists (SUHF-rih-jists) worked for the right to vote. These women had worked for the right to vote since the nation began. In 1920, the Nineteenth Amendment finally passed. This law was added to the U.S. Constitution (kon-stuh-TOO-shuhn). It gave women age 21 and older the right to vote.

The Harlem Renaissance

The early 1900s were hard for African Americans. They did not have the same rights as white people. When shopping, they had to go through different doors. When thirsty, they had to find a "Colored" fountain. They could not drink from "Whites Only" fountains. They could not go to the same schools, either. They had to sit in the backs of buses. They faced segregation (seg-ruh-GAY-shuhn). It was based on their skin color. It was not fair. They had fought for their country in the war. Yet, they were treated badly at home.

In 1909, a group formed. It stood up for the rights of African Americans. It was the National Association for the Advancement of Colored People (NAACP). The NAACP wanted people to know that segregation was wrong. This group is still active today.

In the 1920s, many African Americans left the South. This was called the Great Migration (my-GRAY-shuhn). They moved to the North and the West. They wanted better lives. They settled in cities. They looked for jobs.

One part of New York City is called Harlem. A great renaissance (reh-nuh-SAWNTS) happened there. A renaissance is a time of great change and growth. African American writers, singers, and poets lived in Harlem. They wrote and sang about their lives. Their art touched the lives of other African Americans. Many of the artists of the Harlem Renaissance are still famous. Louis Armstrong was a great trumpet player. Bessie Smith was a singer. Duke Ellington played jazz. Some people call this the start of the Civil Rights Movement.

A Dark Day in History

Many things changed during the first three decades of the 1900s. Women became more active outside of their homes. African Americans succeeded in the arts. People borrowed money. They spent it freely. Many people had cars. They felt successful. The mood in the United States was happy.

But then, the people's moods quickly changed. It happened on October 29, 1929. On Black Tuesday, the stock market crashed. This means that what the stocks were worth dropped. People had borrowed money to buy stocks. Now, those stocks were worth very little. But people still owed money to the banks. The bankers demanded their money plus interest. Interest is extra money paid when people borrow money. But most people did not have the money.

People rushed to the banks to get their money out. When borrowers did not pay back their loans, the banks had no money. They went bankrupt! People lost their life savings. Business after business closed. Companies could not pay their workers. So, people lost their jobs. Those people could not pay for their houses, and they lost them, too. Lots of people were hungry and homeless. The Great Depression (dih-PRESH-uhn) had begun.

Comprehension Question

What were two things that happened during World War I to make women's lives better?

#50084—Leveled Texts: The 20th Century   © Shell Education

The Roaring Twenties

After World War I ended in 1918, the way people lived in the United States changed. This time period is called the Roaring Twenties, and for a while, many Americans were successful. Some of them were rich. People tried new styles of dancing and dressing, and some people rejected traditional morals. They ate, drank, and made merry.

During the war, men were away fighting. So, women did the men's jobs. Before this, some people did not think that women were equal to men, claiming that women were not as smart or as strong. During the war, women proved those people wrong.

Women felt that they should be able to vote just as men could. Women suffragists (SUHF-rih-jists) had been working for the right to vote since the nation began. In 1920, the Nineteenth Amendment passed. This law was added to the U.S. Constitution (kon-stuh-TOO-shuhn). It gave all American women age 21 and older the right to vote.

The Harlem Renaissance

The early 1900s were hard for African Americans. They did not have the same rights as white people. When thirsty, they had to find a "Colored" fountain. They could not drink from fountains marked, "Whites Only." When shopping, African Americans had to go through different doors. They faced unfair segregation (seg-ruh-GAY-shuhn) based on their skin color. They had fought for their country in World War I. Yet, they were treated badly at home.

In 1909, a special group formed. It stood up for the rights of African Americans. The group was named the National Association for the Advancement of Colored People (NAACP). The NAACP wanted people to know that segregation was wrong. This group is still active.

In the 1920s, the Great Migration (my-GRAY-shuhn) took place. Many African Americans moved. They left the South. They went to the North and the West. They hoped to escape segregation. They settled in busy cities and searched for jobs.

One part of New York City is called Harlem. The Harlem Renaissance (reh-nuh-SAWNTS) occurred there. During this time of great change and growth, African American writers, singers, and poets lived there. When they wrote and sang about their lives, they touched the hearts of other African Americans. Many of the Harlem Renaissance artists are still famous. Louis Armstrong was known for his amazing trumpet playing, and Bessie Smith was a singer. Duke Ellington was a jazz musician. Some historians call this the start of the Civil Rights Movement.

A Dark Day in History

Many things changed during the first three decades of the 1900s. Women became more active outside of their homes. African Americans were successful in the arts. People borrowed money. They spent it freely. Many people owned cars. They felt successful. The mood in the United States was happy and carefree.

But, the people's moods quickly changed on October 29, 1929. On this date, called Black Tuesday, the stock market crashed. The value of stocks fell sharply. People had borrowed money to buy valuable stocks. Now, those stocks were worth very little, but people still owed the banks the money they had borrowed. Bankers demanded their money plus interest. But most people did not have the money.

To make matters worse, people were rushing to the banks to get their money out. When borrowers did not pay back their loans, the banks went bankrupt! People lost their savings. Business after business closed. Workers lost their jobs. Without paychecks, people soon lost their homes, too. Lots of people were hungry and homeless. The Great Depression (dih-PRESH-uhn) had begun.

Comprehension Question

Describe how World War I improved life for women.

© Shell Education

The Roaring Twenties

After World War I ended in 1918, the way people lived in the United States changed. This time period is called the Roaring Twenties, and for a while, many Americans felt wealthy and successful. They indulged in new styles of dancing and dressing, and some people rejected traditional moral standards. They ate, drank, and made merry.

During the war, American men were overseas fighting, leaving the women to perform their jobs. Prior to this time, some people thought that women were not equal to men, believing that women were not smart enough or strong enough to do the men's work. During the war, women proved those people wrong.

Women felt that they should be able to vote just as men could. Women suffragists (SUHF-rih-jists) had been trying to get voting rights since the Revolutionary War. In 1920, the Nineteenth Amendment was added to the U.S. Constitution (kon-stuh-TOO-shuhn) and gave all American women age 21 and older the right to vote. Suffragists celebrated this major victory for women.

The Harlem Renaissance

The early 1900s were hard for African Americans. Despite the promises of the U.S. Constitution, they did not have the same rights as white people. African Americans had to enter stores through separate entrances. When thirsty, they could not drink from water fountains that said, "Whites Only." They had to use "Colored" fountains and restrooms. They had to sit in the backs of buses and could not attend the same schools as white children. This segregation (seg-ruh-GAY-shuhn) based on their skin color was unfair. African Americans had fought for their country in World War I, and yet they were treated poorly at home.

In 1909, a special group formed to stand up for the rights of African Americans. This group was named the National Association for the Advancement of Colored People (NAACP), and it is still active today.

In the 1920s, the Great Migration (my-GRAY-shuhn) took place as many African Americans left the South in a quest to escape segregation. Hoping for better opportunities, they moved to the North and the West, settled in busy cities, and searched for jobs.

One section of New York City is called Harlem. The Harlem Renaissance (reh-nuh-SAWNTS), a time of great change and growth, occurred there as African American writers, singers, and poets wrote and sang about their lives. Many of the artists of the Harlem Renaissance are still famous. Louis Armstrong was an amazing trumpet player. Bessie Smith was a famous singer, and Duke Ellington was a well-known jazz musician. Some historians call this the start of the Civil Rights Movement.

A Dark Day in History

Many things changed during the first three decades of the 1900s. Women became more active outside of their homes. African Americans achieved success in the arts. People borrowed money and spent it freely. Many people owned cars and felt successful. The mood in the United States was happy.

But things changed on October 29, 1929. Until then, people had bought stocks with borrowed money. On Black Tuesday, the stock market crashed and stocks' values plummeted. People had borrowed money to buy valuable stocks. Now, those stocks were worth very little, yet people still owed the banks the money they had borrowed. Bankers demanded their money plus interest, but most people did not have the money.

To make matters worse, people rushed to the banks to withdraw their money. When borrowers did not pay back their loans, the banks went bankrupt! People lost their savings. Business after business closed. So, people lost their jobs. Without paychecks, people could not afford their homes. A time of desperation called the Great Depression (dih-PRESH-uhn) had begun.

Comprehension Question

Describe how World War I helped the suffragists.

#50084— *Leveled Texts: The 20th Century*

© Shell Education

The Great Depression

The stock market crashed in October 1929. After that, a lot of companies closed. People lost their jobs. They had lost their savings when the banks closed. So, many people had no money. Families sold all they had. They bought food. But then their cash ran out. They had nothing. Many people felt desperate (DES-puh-ruht). They were scared. They didn't know what to do.

Some people packed up their few belongings. They went from town to town. They looked for jobs. They lived in their cars. If a family did not have a car, they walked. They had to find shelter at night. At times, they slept under bridges. Sometimes, they made shacks. They used old boards and boxes for houses. Getting through the Great Depression (dih-PRESH-uhn) was hard for most Americans. It took the nation a long time to recover.

On the Road

Many farms in the Midwest were no good. There had been a long drought in which little rain fell. So, the land was dry. When the wind blew, it caused dust storms. A lot of Midwest families left their farms. They went west. They hoped life would be good in California. These people were migrants (MY-gruhntz). They were called that since they moved around. But the Californians did not like them. They did not want to compete for jobs. They called the newcomers Okies. Why? Many of them came from the state of Oklahoma.

Most migrants lived in camps. The camps had tents for sleeping. Many people found work on farms in California. They moved from camp to camp. They followed crops. First, they picked cherries. Next, they picked peaches. Then, they picked apples and so on. Life was still hard. But at least they had food.

A New Leader

In 1933, Americans elected Franklin Delano Roosevelt president. He made a famous speech. This was his inaugural (ih-NAW-gyuh-ruhl) speech. It was the first speech he gave as president. President Roosevelt said, "The only thing we have to fear is fear itself." These were brave words in the Great Depression. People trusted him. They thought he could get the country working better.

© Shell Education

#50084—Leveled Texts: The 20th Century

President Roosevelt had a plan. He called it the New Deal. It did not end the depression. But, it helped with some of the problems. It gave Americans hope in democracy. Other nations hit by the depression turned to dictators (DIK-tay-terz) like Hitler. A dictator has complete power and does not allow freedom. The New Deal helped people in need. The government made jobs for people. It paid them to build parks and roads. President Roosevelt did not want children to have to work. He wanted them in school. He wanted everyone to have a home and good food. President Roosevelt's plan lifted the spirits of people.

First Lady Eleanor Roosevelt was a big help. She talked to the American people. She asked them questions. Then, she told her husband what she learned. Without her, President Roosevelt would not have known just what Americans needed.

War Helps the American Economy

By the late 1930s, war had broken out again in Europe. There was fighting in Asia, too. The United States could not live in isolation (i-suh-LAY-shuhn). That meant that it could not ignore the rest of the world. Yet, the United States did not want to join the war. So, President Roosevelt started the Lend-Lease Program. It was a way to help both the United States and other nations. Soon, U.S. factories were making things for the war. Countries overseas needed supplies. They wanted blankets, uniforms, ships, and planes. Making these things meant a lot of jobs for Americans. More people were hired every day.

More women started to work. African Americans were hired. Wages, or pay, got better. Making things for World War II helped to end the Great Depression. America was getting back on its feet.

Comprehension Question

Tell two things President Roosevelt's plan did.

#50084—Leveled Texts: The 20th Century

© Shell Education

The Great Depression

After the stock market crashed in October 1929, a lot of businesses closed. They fired their workers. Without jobs, people had no money, and they had lost their savings when the banks closed. Some families sold all they had to buy food. But when their cash ran out, they had nothing. Many people felt desperate (DES-puh-ruht). They were scared and didn't know what to do.

Some people packed up their few belongings. They left their homes. Many people lived in their cars. If a family did not have a car, they walked. They went from town to town. They had to find shelter at night. Sometimes, they slept under bridges. Other times, they used old boards and boxes for shelter. Getting through the Great Depression (dih-PRESH-uhn) was hard for most Americans. It took the country a long time to recover.

On the Road

Many farms in the Midwest had been ruined by a long drought. A drought means that little rain fell. So, the land was dry. When the wind blew, it caused dust storms. A lot of Midwest families headed west. They thought life would be better in California. These people were migrants (MY-gruhntz). They were called that because they moved around so much. But, the Californians did not like them. The people in California did not want to compete for jobs. So, they called the newcomers Okies. Why? Many of the migrants came from Oklahoma.

Most migrants lived in camps. The camps had tents. The tents were their homes. They could pick up their tents and move from farm to farm. The farms had places to wash. Many of the people found work on farms by following the crops. This meant they moved from camp to camp. They would pick cherries, peaches, and apples. Life was still difficult, but at least they had food to eat.

A New Leader

In 1933, Americans elected Franklin Delano Roosevelt president. He made a famous speech. This was his inaugural (ih-NAW-gyuh-ruhl) speech. It was the first speech he gave as president. President Roosevelt said, "The only thing we have to fear is fear itself." These were brave words during the Great Depression. People trusted him. They thought he could get the country back on track.

71

President Roosevelt had a plan called the New Deal. It did not end the depression, but it helped solve some of the problems. Even more importantly, it gave Americans hope in democracy. Other nations affected by the depression turned to dictators (DIK-tay-tuhrz) like Hitler in Germany. A dictator has complete power and does not allow freedom. The New Deal had laws to help people in need. One government program gave work to people not working by hiring them to build parks and roads. President Roosevelt did not want children to have to work to keep their families going. He wanted the children in school. He wanted everyone to have a home and enough food. His plan lifted Americans' spirits.

First Lady Eleanor Roosevelt was a big help. She went around the country. She talked to Americans. She heard their concerns. Then, she told her husband about the concerns. Without her, President Roosevelt would not have understood exactly what Americans needed.

War Helps the American Economy

By the late 1930s, war had broken out in Europe again. There was fighting in Asia, too. The United States knew it could not live in isolation (i-suh-LAY-shuhn). That meant it could not ignore the rest of the world. Yet, the country did not want to join the war. So, President Roosevelt started the Lend-Lease Program. He saw this as a way to help his own country as well as other nations. Quickly, U.S. factories were busy making things for the war. Countries overseas needed things such as blankets, uniforms, ships, and airplanes. This required a lot of workers, and more jobs were created daily for the United States.

With all these new jobs, more women started to work, and more African Americans were hired. Wages were improving. Wages are what a person earns for doing a job. Making materials for World War II helped to end the Great Depression. America was getting back on its feet.

Comprehension Question

Describe two ways the New Deal helped Americans.

#50084— Leveled Texts: The 20th Century

© Shell Education

The Great Depression

After the stock market crash in October 1929, many businesses were ruined. They fired their workers. Without jobs, the people had no money, and they had lost their savings when the banks closed. To survive, families sold all they had. When their cash ran out, they were penniless. Many people were desperate (DES-puh-ruht).

Some people decided to look for jobs in new towns. They packed up their few belongings and left their homes. Many families lived in their cars. If they did not have a car, the whole family walked from town to town. They had to find shelter each night. Sometimes, they slept under bridges. Other times, they made shelters out of old boards and boxes. Surviving the difficult years of the Great Depression (dih-PRESH-uhn) was very hard for most Americans, and it took the country many years to recover.

On the Road

Many farms in the Midwest had been ruined by a long drought. Without rain, crops were ruined and when the wind blew, dust storms wrecked homes and machinery. So, families headed west, hoping that lives would improve in California. These migrants (MY-gruhntz) were nicknamed Okies by the Californians because many of them came from Oklahoma. The people in California did not like the Okies because they did not want to compete for jobs.

Most migrants lived in camps. The camps had tents for shelter and places to wash. Many migrants found work on farms by following the crops and moving from camp to camp. They would pick cherries, peaches, and apples. Life was still very difficult, but at least they had food to eat.

A New Leader

In 1933, Americans elected Franklin Delano Roosevelt president. He made a famous inaugural (ih-NAW-gyuh-ruhl) speech in which he said, "The only thing we have to fear is fear itself." His brave words during the Great Depression made people trust him. They believed he would get the country back on track.

© Shell Education

#50084—Leveled Texts: The 20th Century

Roosevelt had a plan called the New Deal. It did not end the Depression, but it relieved some of the economic hardship. What's more, it gave Americans faith in democracy at a time when other nations affected by the Depression turned to dictators (DIK-tay-terz) like Hitler. The New Deal had laws to help those in need. One program gave people government jobs building parks and roads. Instead of having young children work to keep their families going, Roosevelt wanted them back in school. He wanted everyone to have a home and food. His plan lifted Americans' spirits.

First Lady Eleanor Roosevelt was a big help as well. She traveled around the country. She talked to the American people. She listened to their concerns, and then told her husband about them. Without her, President Roosevelt would not have understood so clearly what Americans needed.

War Helps the American Economy

By the late 1930s, war had broken out in Europe again. There was fighting in Asia, as well. The United States knew it could not live in isolation (i-suh-LAY-shuhn), but the country did not want to join the war. So, President Roosevelt started the Lend-Lease Program. He saw this as a way to help his own country, too. Soon, factories were busy making products for the war. Countries overseas needed products such as blankets, uniforms, ships, and airplanes. This kind of work required a lot of workers, and more jobs were created daily.

With so many new jobs, more women went to work, too. More African Americans were hired. Wages were increasing. This helped people who had struggled for so long during the Depression. Making materials for World War II helped to end the Great Depression. America was finally getting back on its feet.

Comprehension Question

How did the New Deal lift Americans' spirits?

#50084—Leveled Texts: The 20th Century

© Shell Education

The Great Depression

After the stock market crashed in October 1929, many businesses went bankrupt, leaving lots of people without employment. Without jobs, they had no money coming in, and their savings had vanished when the banks closed. To survive, families sold all they owned just to buy food. When their cash ran out, they had nothing. Many frightened people felt desperate (DES-puh-ruht) and uncertain about what to do.

Some people decided to seek jobs elsewhere. They packed up their few possessions and lived in their cars. If they had no car, the family members walked from place to place. They sought shelter each night, and sometimes they slept under bridges. Other times, they made shelters using old boards and boxes. Surviving the difficult years of the Great Depression (dih-PRESH-uhn) was very hard for most Americans, and it took the economy more than a decade to completely recover.

On the Road

Many farms in the Midwest had been destroyed by a long drought. After years of inadequate rainfall, crops had failed, and all the topsoil was loose. When the wind blew, huge dust storms wrecked homes and machinery. Midwestern families abandoned these farms and headed west, thinking that their lives would improve in California. The Californians nicknamed these migrants (MY-gruhntz) Okies since so many of them came from Oklahoma. It was not a friendly nickname. The people in California did not like the Okies because they did not want to compete for jobs.

Most migrants lived in camps that had tents and places to shower. Many migrants found work on farms by moving from camp to camp, following the crops. They would pick cherries, peaches, and apples. Although life was still difficult, at least they had food to eat.

A New Leader

In 1933, Americans elected Franklin Delano Roosevelt president. In his famous inaugural (ih-NAW-gyuh-ruhl) speech he said, "The only thing we have to fear is fear itself." Making such a bold statement during the Great Depression bolstered people's confidence in him.

75

Roosevelt proposed the New Deal. Although this plan did not end the Depression, it relieved some of the economic problems. Even more importantly, it gave Americans faith in democracy at a time when other nations affected by the Depression turned to dictators (DIK-tay-terz) like Hitler. The New Deal had laws to help those in need. The government gave unemployed people jobs building parks and roads. President Roosevelt wanted children to go back to school instead of working to support their families. He wanted everyone to have a home and enough food. His plan lifted Americans' spirits.

First Lady Eleanor Roosevelt assisted him by traveling around the country and consulting with the American people. She listened to their concerns, and then reported them to her husband. Without her, President Roosevelt would not have understood so clearly exactly what programs Americans needed.

War Helps the American Economy

By the late 1930s, Europe was embroiled in another war, and there was also fighting in Asia. The United States knew that it could not live in isolation (i-suh-LAY-shuhn), but the country did not want to enter the war. So, President Roosevelt started the Lend-Lease Program as a way to help other nations in addition to helping his own. Soon, U.S. factories were busy making products such as blankets, uniforms, ships, and airplanes for the countries overseas. Manufacturing work required a multitude of laborers, and more jobs were created daily.

With so many new jobs, more women and African Americans were hired, and wages increased. Making materials for World War II helped to end the Great Depression. America was finally getting back on its feet.

Comprehension Question

Compare and contrast Roosevelt and the New Deal with dictators from the time period.

© Shell Education

World War II in Europe

Adolf Hitler led Nazi (NOT-see) Germany. He was a dictator. This means that he held all the power in the nation. In 1938, he added Austria (AW-stree-uh) to Germany. Next, Hitler took over Czechoslovakia (chek-uh-slow-VAW-kee-uh).

Hitler wanted to own all of Europe. He planned to take Poland. Both Great Britain and France told him that they would fight back. But, Hitler did not believe them. On September 1, 1939, Hitler's army marched into Poland. This started World War II. On one side was the Axis. This was Germany, Italy, and Japan. On the other side were the Allies. This was Great Britain and France. Soon, Canada and Australia joined the war. They helped the Allies.

The Germans had a war plan. The plan was called blitzkrieg (BLITS-kreeg). First, German planes dropped bombs on the British and French. Then, the German tanks would move in. This caught the Allies by surprise. The Germans bombed British war factories. They bombed the airports. In just two weeks, the Allies were losing. France had to surrender (suh-REN-duhr). This means France gave up. But Great Britain still would not give up. So, Hitler began the Battle of Britain. Each night, German planes dropped bombs. They fell on British cities. British and German planes fought in the sky. The battle lasted more than three months. More than 40,000 British died.

The British saw that they were Europe's last hope. The British did not give up. Hitler knew he had lost the Battle of Britain. For the time being, Hitler gave up on taking over Great Britain.

The Nazis Do Awful Things

Bad things went on in nations Germany had taken over. Each Jewish person had to wear the Star of David. It was a yellow star. It had six points. Hitler's men found the people with the stars. They rounded them up. They forced them to live in crowded, run-down areas called ghettos (GET-toez). The ghettos were crowded. But the Jewish people were not allowed to leave. Many families lived in one building. There was not enough food. There was not enough medicine for the sick.

77

Then, Hitler told the Nazis to put the Jewish people on trains. The trains went to concentration (kon-suhn-TRAY-shuhn) camps. When they arrived, the Nazis split up Jewish husbands, wives, and children. Most Jewish families never saw each other again. The prisoners had to work. Some of them died from working too hard. Others died from hunger. Those who grew weak or sick were killed. There were death camps, too. There, people were killed as they got off the trains. Six million Jewish people died. This was a terrible time called the Holocaust (HOL-uh-kawst).

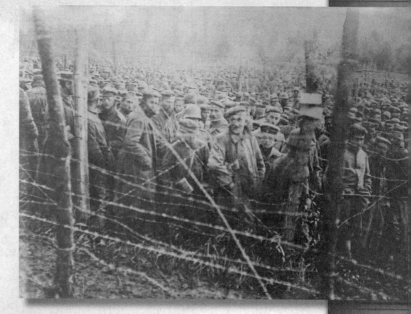

The War

Hitler had promised not to attack the Soviet Union (SOH-vee-et YOON-yuhn). But then, Hitler invaded in June 1941. He said a Soviet loss would show the Allies that he could not be stopped. Hitler would beat the Soviets, too. Hitler thought the Soviets would give up. They did not. In September 1942, the Nazis attacked Stalingrad (STAW-luhn-grad). It was a Soviet city. The Nazis won. But then, the Soviet troops circled the city. They trapped the Germans. Things started to fall apart for the German army.

American troops joined the Allies. They did so after the attack on Pearl Harbor in December 1941. This gave Hitler a new enemy. The Allies had to free France from the Nazis. So, in June 1944, the Allies landed on the beaches of Normandy. This is in France. The Allies made the Nazis back up their troops. The Allies pushed forward. They moved through France. The Nazis kept backing up.

Then, the Allies sent up bomber planes. They dropped bombs on German cities. For the first time, Germany was under attack. Hitler made old men and young boys fight. He told them to defend Berlin, the capital. But by then, the Soviets had already reached Berlin. Hitler knew that he had lost. He killed himself.

The Germans gave up on May 8, 1945. The war in Europe had ended. But it was still going on in the Pacific.

Comprehension Question

What is blitzkrieg?

#50084—Leveled Texts: The 20th Century

© Shell Education

World War II in Europe

Adolf Hitler was the leader of Nazi (NOT-see) Germany. He was a dictator. A dictator has all the power for the whole country. In 1938, he took over Austria (AW-stree-uh) and made it part of Germany. Next, Hitler took over Czechoslovakia (chek-uh-slow-VAW-kee-uh).

Hitler wanted to own all of Europe. He planned to take Poland next. This time, both Great Britain and France told him that they would fight back if he tried. But, Hitler did not think that they would act. On September 1, 1939, he invaded Poland. This started World War II. On one side was the Axis. The Axis was made up of Germany, Italy, and Japan. On the other side were the Allies of Great Britain and France. Soon other nations, such as Canada and Australia, joined the Allies.

The Germans used a plan called blitzkrieg (BLITS-kreeg). First, German planes dropped bombs on the British and French. Then, the German tanks moved in. This caught Great Britain and France by surprise. The Germans bombed British aircraft factories and airfields. In just two weeks, the Allies were on the run. France had to give up and surrender (suh-REN-duhr). Hitler knew that Great Britain could keep him from ruling Europe. He began the Battle of Britain. Night after night, the Germans dropped bombs on British cities. German and British planes fought in the sky. The battle lasted for more than three months. More than 40,000 British people died.

The British knew that they were Europe's last hope. They would not give up. Hitler knew he had lost the Battle of Britain. His planes could not defeat the Royal Air Force of Britain. For the time being, Hitler gave up on overpowering Great Britain.

The Nazis Do Awful Things

Meanwhile, in German-held countries, each Jewish person had to wear the Star of David. It was a yellow star with six points. This made it easy for Hitler's secret police to round the Jewish people up and move them to poor neighborhoods called ghettos (GET-toez). In the ghettos, food and medicine were hard to find. Many people died of hunger and illness.

79

Then, Hitler sent Jewish people to concentration (kon-suhn-TRAY-shuhn) camps. In the concentration camps, the Nazis split up husbands, wives, and children. Most Jewish families never saw each other again. The prisoners had to work. A lot of people died from hunger. Others died from working too hard. Those who grew too weak or sick to work were killed. In death camps, people were killed as they got off the trains. About six million Jewish people died in these camps. This terrible time is called the Holocaust (HOL-uh-kawst).

The War

Hitler promised not to attack the Soviet Union (SOH-vee-et YOON-yuhn). But then, he attacked it in June 1941. He felt that if he could beat the Soviet Union, it would show the Allies that he could not be stopped. Hitler thought the Soviets would give up. But he was wrong. In September 1942, the Nazis attacked the Soviet city of Stalingrad (STAW-luhn-grad). The Germans won. But then, the Soviet troops surrounded them. They trapped the Germans in the city. Things started to fall apart for the German army.

American troops joined the Allies after the attack on Pearl Harbor in December 1941. This gave Hitler a new, strong enemy. The Allies had to liberate, or free, France from the Nazis. So, in June 1944, the Allies landed on the beaches of Normandy. This is in France. The Allies made the Nazis back up. Inch by inch, the Allies pushed forward. They moved through the mainland of France. The Nazis left.

Then, the Allies sent bomber planes over German cities. They dropped bombs. The cities were being ruined. Hitler forced elderly men and young boys to fight. He told them to defend Berlin, the capital. But, the Soviets had already reached this city.

When Hitler knew that he had lost, he killed himself. The Germans gave up on May 8, 1945. The war had ended in Europe. But, it was still going on in the Pacific.

Comprehension Question

Describe the German plan of blitzkrieg.

#50084— Leveled Texts: The 20th Century

© Shell Education

World War II in Europe

Adolf Hitler was the dictator of Nazi (NOT-see) Germany. In 1938, he merged Austria (AW-stree-uh) with Germany. Next, Hitler decided to take over Czechoslovakia (chek-uh-slow-VAW-kee-uh). He reminded the public that before World War I, it had been part of Germany. His army took over that country, too.

Actually, Hitler wanted to control all of Europe. He planned to take Poland next. This time, both Great Britain and France warned him that they would fight back. Hitler believed they would not act to stop him. On September 1, 1939, Hitler invaded Poland and started World War II. On one side was the Axis made up of the nations of Germany, Italy, and Japan. On the other side were the Allies of Great Britain and France. Soon other nations, such as Canada and Australia, joined the Allies.

The Germans used a tactic called *blitzkrieg* (BLITS-kreeg) against the British and French. First, German planes dropped bombs on them. Then, the German army moved in with tanks. The blitzkrieg caught Great Britain and France off guard. The Germans started bombing British aircraft factories and airfields. In just two weeks, the Allies were on the run. France had to surrender (suh-REN-duhr). Hitler knew that only Great Britain could stop him from ruling Europe. The Battle of Britain began. Night after night, the Germans dropped bombs on British cities. German and British planes fought in the sky. More than 40,000 British people died.

Knowing that they were Europe's only hope, the British refused to give up. After more than three months of fighting, Hitler knew that he had lost the Battle of Britain. His planes could not defeat the Royal Air Force. For the time being, he gave up on overpowering Great Britain.

The Nazis Do Awful Things

Meanwhile, in the German-controlled countries, every Jewish person had to wear the Star of David. This yellow star with six points made it easy for Hitler's secret police to round up the Jewish people and move them to ghettos (GET-toez). In the ghettos, food and medicine were scarce. Many people died from hunger and illness.

81

Then, Hitler started to send Jewish people to concentration (kon-suhn-TRAY-shuhn) camps. There, the Nazis separated husbands from wives and children. Most never saw each other again. The prisoners had to work. Many people died from exhaustion or starvation. When prisoners grew too weak or sick to work, they were killed. In death camps, people were killed as soon as they got off the trains. About six million Jewish people died in these horrible camps. This tragedy is called the Holocaust (HOL-uh-kawst).

The War

Hitler decided to attack the Soviet Union (SOH-vee-et YOON-yuhn) in June 1941. He did this after he had promised not to attack them. Hitler felt that a Soviet defeat would show the Allies that Germany was unstoppable. Hitler thought the Soviets would give up easily, but he was wrong. In September 1942, the Nazis attacked the Soviet city of Stalingrad (STAW-luhn-grad). Although the Nazis won, the Soviets surrounded the city, trapping the German troops. Things started to fall apart for the German army.

American troops joined the Allies after the attack on Pearl Harbor in December 1941. This gave Hitler a new, strong enemy. The Allies knew they had to liberate, or free, France from the Nazis. In June 1944, the Allies stormed the beaches of Normandy, France. The Allies overwhelmed the Nazis. Over the next few months, the Allies fought battles through the mainland of France. The Nazis fled.

Then, the Allies sent bomber planes to destroy German cities. For the first time, the German homeland was under attack. Hitler made elderly men and young boys take up arms and fight. Although Hitler told them to defend their capital, Berlin, it was hopeless. The Soviets were already there. Hitler killed himself, and the Germans surrendered on May 8, 1945. The war was over in Europe, but it still raged in the Pacific.

Comprehension Question

Explain why blitzkrieg was a good plan.

#50084— Leveled Texts: The 20th Century

© Shell Education

World War II in Europe

Adolf Hitler was the dictator of Nazi (NOT-see) Germany. In 1938, he merged Austria (AW-stree-uh) with Germany. Next, Hitler invaded Czechoslovakia (chek-uh-slow-VAW-kee-uh) after reminding the public that prior to World War I, it had belonged to Germany.

Hitler, who wanted to control all of Europe, planned to take Poland next. This time, both Great Britain and France warned him that they would fight back, but Hitler believed they would not attempt to stop him. On September 1, 1939, Hitler invaded Poland, and World War II began. On one side was the Axis, consisting of the nations of Germany, Italy, and Japan. On the other side were the Allies of Great Britain and France. Soon other nations, such as Canada and Australia, joined the Allies.

The Germans used a tactic called blitzkrieg (BLITS-kreeg). First, German planes dropped bombs on an area, and then German tanks moved in. The blitzkrieg caught the British and French by surprise. The Germans began bombing British aircraft factories and airfields. In just two weeks, the Allies were on the run, and France had to surrender (suh-REN-duhr). Hitler realized that only Great Britain stood in his way of ruling Europe, and he began the Battle of Britain. Night after night, German aircraft bombed British cities. Intense battles took place between German and British planes. More than 40,000 British died.

Knowing that they were Europe's only hope, the British refused to surrender, and after more than three months of fighting, Hitler knew that he had lost the Battle of Britain. Great Britain's Royal Air Force was undefeatable, so for the time being, Hitler gave up trying to overpower them.

The Nazis Do Awful Things

Meanwhile, in German-controlled countries, every Jewish person had to wear the Star of David. This made it easy for Hitler's secret police to round up the Jewish people and move them to ghettos (GET-toez). In the ghettos, food and medicine were scarce, and many people died of starvation or disease.

83

Then, Hitler told the Nazis to exterminate, or murder, all the Jewish people. They packed them into trains and sent them to concentration (kon-suhn-TRAY-shuhn) camps. There, husbands, wives, and children were separated, and most of them never saw each other again. The Jewish prisoners worked until they died from exhaustion or starvation. People who grew too weak or sick to work were killed. In the death camps, people were murdered shortly after they stepped off the trains. Around six million Jewish people perished in these horrible camps. This terrible tragedy is called the Holocaust (HOL-uh-kawst).

The War

Hitler invaded the Soviet Union (SOH-vee-et YOON-yuhn) in June 1941, after promising not to attack it. He felt that a Soviet defeat would prove to the Allies that Germany was unstoppable and make them surrender. Hitler thought the Soviets would give up, but he was wrong. In September 1942, the Nazis attacked the Soviet city of Stalingrad (STAW-luhn-grad) and won. However, the Soviets surrounded the city and trapped the German troops. The tide was turning against the Nazis.

American soldiers had joined the Allies after the attack on Pearl Harbor in December 1941, giving Hitler another strong enemy. The Allies had to liberate, or free, France from Nazi control. In June 1944, tens of thousands of Allies stormed the beaches of Normandy, France. By the end of the first day, the Allies had overwhelmed the Nazis. Over the next few months, the Allies fought fierce battles to advance through the mainland of France. The Nazis retreated.

Then, the Allies sent bomber planes over German cities, putting the German homeland under siege for the first time. Hitler forced elderly men and little boys to take up weapons. Although he urged them to defend their capital city of Berlin, it was hopeless. The Soviets were already there. When Hitler realized this, he committed suicide. The Germans surrendered on May 8, 1945, ending World War II in Europe. However, the war still raged in the Pacific.

Comprehension Question

Describe at least two reasons why the blitzkrieg was not successful.

#50084—*Leveled Texts: The 20th Century*

© Shell Education

World War II in the Pacific

WINDSOR ELEMENTARY SCHOOL MEDIA CENTER

Japan invaded China in 1937. The United States did not like this. U.S. President Roosevelt spoke up. He said that he would not sell Japan oil or steel. Japan needed these things to fight the war. Japan wanted to take over other nations in East Asia to get the oil. So, President Roosevelt put bomber planes in the Philippines to protect these nations. The Philippines are islands. They are between Japan and the nations with the oil. The president sent ships, too. He had them go to Pearl Harbor. Pearl Harbor is in Hawaii. These actions upset the Japanese.

Surprise Attack!

It was Sunday, December 7, 1941. Hundreds of Japanese planes sat on ships. The ships were in the Pacific Ocean. The planes were there to bomb Pearl Harbor. Pearl Harbor was a big U.S. navy base. It had the most U.S. forces in the Pacific. The Japanese planes took off. It was just before 8:00 A.M. The Japanese started dropping bombs. The Americans were caught off guard. In just two hours, the Japanese ruined 188 aircraft. They sank 21 ships. More than 2,400 Americans died.

Japan saw this attack as a success. On the same day, Japan also hit the Philippines. Japan hoped to make the United States leave the Pacific. The next day, the United States and Great Britain declared war on Japan. Three days later, Germany and Italy declared war on the United States. Why? They were part of the Axis. The Axis was made up of Japan, Germany, and Italy. The Axis nations were against the Allies. The Allies included Great Britain and France. The United States joined the Allies.

The Battle of Midway

By June 1942, the Japanese attacked a U.S. base. The U.S. base was on Midway, a small island in the Pacific. A win there could put the Japanese in charge of the Pacific. Then, they could strike the West Coast of the United States. The Japanese thought it would be a surprise. But U.S. code breakers had found out about the plan. The United States sent up planes, fought hard, and won the battle.

© Shell Education

#50084—Leveled Texts: The 20th Century

The Bloody Battle of Iwo Jima

The Americans wanted to control a small island. The island was named Iwo Jima (ee-WOH JEE-muh). Iwo Jima stood in the way of reaching the Japanese mainland. Planes from the island shot down U.S. planes. The United States wanted this island to be a base for U.S. planes. The United States attacked the island.

There was a Japanese commander on the island. He asked for reinforcements (ree-uhn-FORS-muhntz). This means he asked Japan for more troops. But no troops were sent by Japan. He knew he would lose the battle. Still, he told his men to fight to their deaths. They must not give up.

The awful battle lasted 34 days. Both sides lost many men. Thousands died. Thousands were hurt. The Americans won. They had a new base in the Pacific. From there, they could send up planes. They could drop bombs on Japan. The Japanese had started a war in America. Now, America would bring the war to the Japanese homeland.

The War Ends

Scientists had made an atomic bomb. U.S. President Harry Truman chose to use it. The bomb fell on August 6, 1945. It landed on Hiroshima (huh-ROH-shuh-muh). The bomb wiped out the city. More than 70,000 people died. But Japan did not surrender (suh-REN-duhr). They did not give up. So, another atomic bomb fell three days later. It hit the city of Nagasaki (nah-gah-SAH-kee). Another 40,000 died. Then, the Japanese gave up. They surrendered (suh-REN-duhrd). World War II was over. More people had died in this war than in any war before.

Comprehension Question

Why did Americans want to control Iwo Jima?

© Shell Education

World War II in the Pacific

Japan attacked China in 1937. The United States did not like this. U.S. President Roosevelt told Japanese leaders that he would not sell them oil or steel. Japan needed these things to fight the war. Japan wanted to take over other nations in East Asia to get the oil. So, Roosevelt put bomber planes in the Philippine Islands. These islands are between Japan and the nations with the oil. President Roosevelt sent ships, too. These ships went to Pearl Harbor in Hawaii. His actions angered the Japanese.

Surprise Attack!

On Sunday, December 7, 1941, hundreds of Japanese planes sat on ships in the Pacific Ocean. These Japanese planes planned to bomb Pearl Harbor. Pearl Harbor was a big U.S. naval base. It had the most U.S. forces in the Pacific. The Japanese planes took off. They began dropping bombs just before 8:00 A.M. The Americans were taken by surprise. In less than two hours, the Japanese had ruined 188 U.S. aircraft. They had sunk 21 U.S. ships. More than 2,400 Americans died.

Japan saw its attack on Pearl Harbor as a success. On the same day, Japan also hit the Philippine Islands. Japan hoped to knock the United States out of the Pacific. The next day, the United States and Great Britain declared war on Japan. Three days later, Germany and Italy declared war on the United States. This was because they were part of the Axis. The Axis was made up of Japan, Germany, and Italy. The Axis nations were against the Allies. The Allies included Great Britain and France. The United States joined the Allies.

The Battle of Midway

In June 1942, the Japanese attacked the U.S. base on Midway. Midway is a small Pacific island. A win there could give the Japanese control over the Pacific. Then, Japan could strike the West Coast of the United States. The Japanese counted on it being a surprise. But, U.S. code breakers had found out what was planned. The United States forces prepared their planes. The United States fought back and won the battle.

© Shell Education

The Bloody Battle of Iwo Jima

The Japanese knew the Americans wanted the small island of Iwo Jima (ee-WOH JEE-muh). Why? Iwo Jima stood in the way of the United States attacking the Japanese mainland. Japanese planes took off from the island. Then, they shot down U.S. planes. The United States wanted to control the island.

The Japanese commander on the island asked for reinforcements (ree-uhn-FORS-muhntz). This means that he needed more troops. He was told that no more troops were coming. He knew Japan would lose the island. Still, he told his men to fight to their deaths. No matter what, they could not give up.

This awful battle lasted 34 days. Thousands of men died on both sides. When it was over, the Americans had won. They had a new base in the Pacific. From there, they could launch planes. They could drop bombs on Japan. The Japanese had started a war in America. Now, America would bring the war to the Japanese homeland.

The War Ends

U.S. scientists had made an atomic bomb. President Harry Truman decided to use it. The bomb fell on August 6, 1945. It landed on Hiroshima (huh-ROH-shuh-muh). It wiped out the city. More than 70,000 people died. But Japan did not surrender (suh-REN-duhr). So, another atomic bomb fell three days later. It hit the city of Nagasaki (nah-gah-SAH-kee). Another 40,000 people died. Then, the Japanese gave up. World War II was over. More people had died in this war than in any war before.

Comprehension Question

Why did the Japanese defend Iwo Jima?

#50084— *Leveled Texts: The 20th Century*

© *Shell Education*

World War II in the Pacific

Japan invaded China in 1937. The United States did not like this. So, U.S. President Roosevelt told Japanese leaders that America would not sell them oil or steel. They needed these things to fight the war. Japan decided to take over other nations in East Asia to get oil. To prevent this, Roosevelt stationed bomber planes in the Philippines. The Philippines are between Japan and the nations with oil. The president sent ships to Pearl Harbor in Hawaii, too. His actions frustrated the Japanese.

Surprise Attack!

Early on Sunday, December 7, 1941, hundreds of planes waited on Japanese ships in the Pacific Ocean. They planned to bomb Pearl Harbor, a large U.S. naval base. It had the biggest group of U.S. forces in the Pacific. The Japanese planes began bombing just before 8:00 A.M. The Americans were taken completely by surprise, and in less than two hours, the Japanese had ruined 188 U.S. aircraft and 21 ships. More than 2,400 Americans died.

Japan saw its attack on Pearl Harbor as a success. On the same day, Japan also attacked the Philippines in an attempt to knock the United States out of the Pacific. The attack made Americans angry. The next day, the United States and Great Britain declared war on Japan. Three days later, Germany and Italy declared war on the United States. This happened because they were part of the Axis. The Axis was made up of Japan, Germany, and Italy. The Axis nations were against the Allies. The Allies included Great Britain and France. The United States joined the Allies.

The Battle of Midway

In June 1942, the Japanese attacked the U.S. base on Midway, a tiny Pacific island. A victory there would give the Japanese control over the Pacific. Then, they could attack the western United States. The Japanese counted on a surprise attack, but U.S. code breakers had discovered their plans. The United States forces readied their planes, fought back, and won the battle.

89

The Bloody Battle of Iwo Jima

The small island of Iwo Jima (ee-WOH JEE-muh) stood in the way of the Americans attacking the Japanese mainland. The Japanese knew the Americans would try to take this island. The Japanese commander on the island asked for reinforcements (ree-uhn-FORS-muhntz). When he heard none were coming, he knew Japan would lose the island. Still, he gave his men orders not to surrender and to fight to their deaths.

As a result, the terrible battle lasted 34 days. Thousands of men died on both sides. When it was over, the Americans had won a base in the Pacific. From there, they could launch planes to drop bombs on Japan. The Japanese had started a war in America. Now, America would bring the war to the Japanese homeland.

The War Ends

U.S. scientists had created a powerful atomic bomb. President Harry Truman decided to use it. The bomb fell on August 6, 1945. It landed on Hiroshima (huh-ROH-shuh-muh) and wiped out the city. More than 70,000 people died. But Japan did not surrender (suh-REN-duhr). So, another atomic bomb fell three days later on the city of Nagasaki (nah-gah-SAH-kee). Another 40,000 people died. Then, the Japanese surrendered. World War II, the deadliest war in history, was over.

Comprehension Question

What were the benefits of having control of Iwo Jima? Describe both the American and Japanese points of view.

#50084—Leveled Texts: The 20th Century

© Shell Education

World War II in the Pacific

In 1937, Japan invaded China. The United States felt this was wrong, and U.S. President Roosevelt told Japanese leaders that America would not sell them oil or steel. Since the Japanese needed oil to fight the war, they decided to conquer other nations in Asia to obtain it. To prevent this, Roosevelt stationed bomber planes in the Philippines, which are between Japan and the nations with the oil. The president also sent battleships to Pearl Harbor in Hawaii. His actions frustrated the Japanese, and they decided to launch an attack on America.

Surprise Attack!

Early on Sunday, December 7, 1941, hundreds of planes waited on Japanese ships in the Pacific Ocean. They planned to bomb Pearl Harbor, a large naval base with the biggest group of U.S. forces in the Pacific. The Japanese planes began bombing just before 8:00 A.M. and caught the Americans completely off guard. In less than two hours, the Japanese had ruined 188 U.S. aircraft and 21 ships and killed more than 2,400 Americans.

Japan saw its attack on Pearl Harbor as a success. On the same day, it also attacked the Philippines in an attempt to knock the United States out of the Pacific. The attack had made Americans angry and determined. The next day, the United States and Great Britain declared war on Japan. Three days later, Germany and Italy declared war on the United States. This happened because these nations were part of the Axis powers made up of Japan, Germany, and Italy. The Axis nations were against the Allies. The Allies included Great Britain and France. The United States joined the Allies.

The Battle of Midway

In June 1942, the Japanese attacked the U.S. base on Midway, a tiny Pacific island. A victory there would give the Japanese control over the Pacific so that they could attack the western United States. The Japanese counted on a surprise attack, but U.S. code breakers had discovered what was planned. The U.S. forces readied their planes, fought back, and won the battle.

91

The Bloody Battle of Iwo Jima

The small island of Iwo Jima (ee-WOH JEE-muh) stood in the way of the Americans attacking the Japanese mainland. The Japanese knew the Americans would try to take this island, so the Japanese commander on the island asked for reinforcements (ree-uhn-FORS-muhntz). When he heard none were coming, he knew he would lose the island. Still, he told his men to not surrender and to fight to their deaths.

As a result, the terrible battle lasted 34 days and killed thousands of men on both sides. When it was over, the Americans had won a base in the Pacific from which they could launch planes to drop bombs on Japan. The Japanese had started a war in America. Now, America would bring the war to the Japanese homeland.

The War Ends

U.S. scientists had created a powerful atomic bomb, and President Harry Truman decided to use it. When the bomb fell on August 6, 1945, on Hiroshima (huh-ROH-shuh-muh), it wiped out the city and killed more than 70,000 people. Even so, Japan did not surrender (suh-REN-duhr) until after a second atomic bomb was dropped three days later on the city of Nagasaki (nah-gah-SAH-kee). Another 40,000 people died. World War II, the deadliest war in history, was finally over.

Comprehension Question

Why was it important for Americans to take the war to Japan's homeland?

#50084— *Leveled Texts: The 20th Century*

© *Shell Education*

World War II Leaders

Churchill and Hitler

Winston Churchill was a British army leader. He was worried. World War I had ended with a treaty. A treaty is an agreement. This treaty was called the Treaty of Versailles (vuhr-SI). Winston Churchill felt that this treaty would cause a new war. He was right.

Now, it was 1933. Adolf Hitler was the ruler of Nazi (NOT-see) Germany. He added more men to the German army. This was against the treaty. Churchill wanted Great Britain to make a pact, or deal, with France and the Soviet (SOH-vee-et) Union. The three nations would stand together. Then, Hitler would back down. A prime minister named Neville Chamberlain led Great Britain. Chamberlain did not act on Churchill's idea of a pact.

In 1938, Hitler made Austria (AW-stree-uh) part of Germany. Churchill saw that Hitler planned to own Europe. Next, Hitler took over Czechoslovakia (chek-uh-slow-VAW-kee-uh). Hitler's army just marched in. Not one shot was fired. It looked like no one would stop Hitler.

Hitler wanted to have Poland, too. Prime Minister Chamberlain said he would defend Poland. Hitler did not believe him. But Hitler did think a threat stood in his way. This threat was the Soviet leader. His name was Joseph Stalin. Hitler said he would not invade the Soviet Union. (He later broke his promise.) Stalin said that he would not try to stop Hitler. On September 1, 1939, Hitler marched into Poland. Great Britain declared war on Germany. World War II had begun.

In 1940, Winston Churchill became the British prime minister. He was a great leader. Mr. Churchill gave his people hope. They faced a strong enemy. Without Churchill, the outcome of the war could have been quite different.

© Shell Education

#50084—Leveled Texts: The 20th Century

Roosevelt and Truman

U.S. President Franklin D. Roosevelt wanted to help nations that fought the Axis powers. The Axis powers were made up of Germany, Italy, and Japan. Roosevelt gave "all aid short of war." Why? He felt that an Axis win would hurt democracy. Still, Americans did not want to join the war.

Then, the Japanese attacked the United States. A few days later, Germany declared war on the United States. The United States had to fight. It had to fight in two places in the world at once.

President Roosevelt served four terms. He was the only U.S. president elected so many times. He was brave and wise. But, he died suddenly in 1945. That made Harry S. Truman the U.S. president. Truman faced a big decision. Should he drop an atomic bomb on Japan? It would save the lives of tens of thousands of U.S. men. He chose to use the bomb.

Emperor Hirohito

Emperor Hirohito (hear-oh-HEE-tow) ruled Japan. He led the nation from 1926 to 1989. At first, his people thought he wanted peace. But in 1937, Japan invaded China. A few years later, Japan joined the Axis. This meant Japan joined in World War II. In the end, it cost three million Japanese lives.

After the two atomic bombs, Emperor Hirohito knew that he had to give up. But first, he made a deal. He said he would get his people to agree to peace. In return, he did not have to stand trial for his part in the war.

Comprehension Question

What happened when Hitler marched into Poland?

94

© Shell Education

World War II Leaders

Churchill and Hitler

Winston Churchill was a British army leader. He had warned people that World War I's Treaty of Versailles (vuhr-SI) would cause a new war. He was right. In 1933, Adolf Hitler became the leader of Nazi (NOT-see) Germany. Hitler said that he would break the treaty. He broke the treaty by rebuilding the German army. Churchill wanted Great Britain to make a pact with France and the Soviet (SOH-vee-et) Union. A pact is an agreement. The three nations would work together. Then, hopefully Hitler would back down. Great Britain's prime minister was Neville Chamberlain. He did not make the pact with France and the Soviet Union.

In 1938, Hitler made Austria (AW-stree-uh) part of Germany. Chamberlain did nothing. But, Churchill knew that Hitler planned to take over Europe. Next, Hitler took over Czechoslovakia (chek-uh-slow-VAW-kee-uh). The German army just marched in. Not one shot was fired. Churchill was upset. It looked like Great Britain would not stop Hitler.

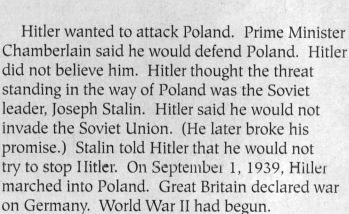

Hitler wanted to attack Poland. Prime Minister Chamberlain said he would defend Poland. Hitler did not believe him. Hitler thought the threat standing in the way of Poland was the Soviet leader, Joseph Stalin. Hitler said he would not invade the Soviet Union. (He later broke his promise.) Stalin told Hitler that he would not try to stop Hitler. On September 1, 1939, Hitler marched into Poland. Great Britain declared war on Germany. World War II had begun.

In 1940, Winston Churchill became the British prime minister. His leadership was important. He gave the British people hope. They had to face a strong enemy. Without him, the outcome of the war could have been quite different.

© Shell Education

#50084—Leveled Texts: The 20th Century

Roosevelt and Truman

U.S. President Franklin D. Roosevelt gave "all aid short of war" to nations that fought the Axis powers. The Axis was Germany, Italy, and Japan. President Roosevelt felt that an Axis win would hurt democracy. Still, Americans did not want to enter the war. Then, the Japanese attacked the United States. A few days later, Germany declared war on the United States. The nation had to fight back. And, it had to fight in two places in the world at once.

Roosevelt was the only U.S. president ever elected to four terms in office. He was brave and wise. He died suddenly in 1945. Harry S. Truman was Roosevelt's vice president. After Roosevelt's death, Truman was in charge. Truman faced a big decision: Should he drop an atomic bomb on Japan? It would save the lives of tens of thousands of U.S. troops. He chose to drop the bomb.

Emperor Hirohito

Japan's Emperor Hirohito (hear-oh-HEE-tow) led the nation from 1926 to 1989. At first, his people thought he was peaceful. But in 1937, Japan invaded China. Just a few years later, Japan joined the Axis. This meant the nation entered World War II. By the end, it had cost three million Japanese lives.

After the two atomic bombs fell, Emperor Hirohito knew that he had to give up. But first, he made a deal. He promised to get his people to agree to a peace treaty. In return, he did not have to stand trial for his part in the war.

Comprehension Question

What event started World War II?

#50084— *Leveled Texts: The 20th Century*   © *Shell Education*

World War II Leaders

Churchill and Hitler

Winston Churchill was a British military leader. He had warned people that World War I's Treaty of Versailles (vuhr-SI) would cause another war. He was right. In 1933, Adolf Hitler became the leader of Nazi (NOT-see) Germany. Hitler boldly announced that he would break the treaty. He would rebuild the German army. Churchill wanted Great Britain to form a pact with France and the Soviet (SOH-vee-et) Union. He hoped the three countries could present a united front. Then, Hitler would back down. But, Great Britain's Prime Minister Neville Chamberlain ignored Churchill's suggestion.

In 1938, Hitler merged Austria (AW-stree-uh) with Germany. Chamberlain did nothing. However, Churchill knew that Hitler planned to continue taking over Europe. Hitler took over Czechoslovakia (chek-uh-slow-VAW-kee-uh). The German army marched into that nation without a single shot fired. Churchill was outraged. It appeared that Great Britain would not stop Hitler.

Hitler planned to attack Poland next. Prime Minister Chamberlain said he would defend Poland. Hitler did not take him seriously. He thought the threat standing in the way of Poland was the Russian leader, Joseph Stalin. Hitler promised not to invade the Soviet Union. (He later broke his promise.) Stalin told Hitler that he would not interfere. On September 1, 1939, Hitler invaded Poland. This forced Great Britain to declare war. World War II had officially begun.

In 1940, Winston Churchill became the British prime minister. His leadership was important throughout World War II. He encouraged the British people as they fought against a powerful enemy. Without him, the outcome of the war could have been quite different.

Roosevelt and Truman

Between 1939 and 1941, U.S. President Franklin D. Roosevelt gave "all aid short of war" to nations fighting the Axis powers of Germany, Italy, and Japan. He felt that an Axis victory would endanger democracy everywhere. However, Americans did not want to get involved in the war. Then, the Japanese attacked the United States. A few days later, Germany declared war on the United States. The nation had to fight back—and on two sides of the world at the same time.

Roosevelt was the only U.S. president ever elected to four terms in office. He was a brave and wise leader. He died suddenly in 1945. Harry S. Truman was Roosevelt's vice president. After Roosevelt's death, Truman was in charge. Truman faced a big decision: Should he drop the atomic bomb on Japan? He knew that it would save tens of thousands of U.S. soldiers' lives if he did so. He chose to drop the bomb.

Emperor Hirohito

Japan's Emperor Hirohito (hear-oh-HEE-tow) led the nation from 1926 to 1989. At first, his people thought he was a peaceful man. But in 1937, his country invaded China. Just a few years later, he formed an alliance with Germany and Italy. This meant his nation entered World War II and ended up costing about three million Japanese lives.

After the two atomic bombs fell, Hirohito knew that he had to surrender, but first he made a deal with the United States. He promised to get his people to support a peace treaty. In return, he did not have to stand trial for his part in the war.

Comprehension Question

What made Hitler think that Chamberlain would let him invade Poland?

#50084—*Leveled Texts: The 20th Century*

© *Shell Education*

World War II Leaders

Churchill and Hitler

Winston Churchill was a British military leader. He warned people that World War I's Treaty of Versailles (vuhr-SI) would cause another war, and he was right. When Adolf Hitler became the leader of Nazi (NOT-see) Germany in 1933, he boldly announced that he would break the treaty by rebuilding the German army. Churchill urged Great Britain to form a pact with France and the Soviet (SOH-vee-et) Union in the hopes that presenting a strong front from the three countries would make Hitler back down. But, Great Britain's Prime Minister Neville Chamberlain ignored Churchill's suggestion.

In 1938, Hitler merged Austria (AW-stree-uh) with Germany, but Chamberlain did nothing. Churchill realized that Hitler planned to seize control of the European continent. Next, Hitler decided to take over Czechoslovakia (chek-uh-slow-VAW-kee-uh). The German army marched into the nation without a single shot fired. Churchill was outraged because it appeared that Great Britain would not attempt to stop Hitler.

Hitler planned to attack Poland next, even though Prime Minister Chamberlain said he would defend Poland. Hitler did not take him seriously and believed the only threat standing in the way of Poland was the Soviet leader, Joseph Stalin. Hitler promised not to invade the Soviet Union—a promise he later broke. Stalin told Hitler that he would not interfere in Poland. So, on September 1, 1939, Hitler invaded Poland, forcing Great Britain to declare war on Germany and officially beginning World War II.

In 1940, Winston Churchill became the British prime minister. His leadership was important as he encouraged the British people to face a powerful and determined enemy. Without him, the outcome of the war could have been very different.

99

Roosevelt and Truman

Between 1939 and 1941, U.S. President Franklin D. Roosevelt gave "all aid short of war" to the nations fighting the Axis powers of Germany, Italy, and Japan. He felt that an Axis victory would jeopardize democracy worldwide. However, Americans did not want to participate in the conflict. After the Japanese attacked the United States, Germany declared war on the United States. Then, the nation had to fight back—and on two sides of the world simultaneously.

Roosevelt was the only U.S. president ever elected to four terms in office. He was a brave and wise leader, but he died suddenly in 1945. Harry S. Truman was Roosevelt's vice president. After Roosevelt's death, Truman was in charge. Truman faced a big decision: Should he drop the atomic bomb on Japan? He knew that it would save tens of thousands of U.S. soldiers' lives if he did so. He made the fateful decision to drop the bomb.

Emperor Hirohito

Japan's Emperor Hirohito (hear-oh-HEE-tow) led the nation from 1926 to 1989. At first, his people thought he was a peaceful man. But in 1937, his country invaded China, and just a few years later, he formed an alliance with Germany and Italy. Joining the Axis meant that he committed his nation to fighting in World War II. By the end of the war, it had cost three million Japanese lives.

After the two atomic bombs fell, Hirohito knew that he had to surrender, but first he made a deal with the United States. He promised to get his people to support a peace treaty if he did not have to stand trial for his part in the war.

Comprehension Question

Why was Churchill viewed as a stronger leader than Chamberlain?

#50084— Leveled Texts: The 20th Century

© Shell Education

The Civil Rights Movement

There used to be laws that stopped some people from drinking at some water fountains. They could not eat at some restaurants. On a bus, they had to sit in the back. Why? Because their skin color was black. This is called segregation (seg-rih-GAY-shuhn). Segregation is how things used to be in parts of the United States. Segregation was very bad in the South. Then, some brave people decided things had to change. These brave people began the Civil Rights Movement. Things started to get better.

Oliver Brown wanted his daughter to go to the school closest to their home. But his daughter was an African American. The nearby school was just for white children. The National Association for the Advancement of Colored People (NAACP) offered to help. It sued the school district in court. It tried to get the child into the white school. The lawsuit was *Brown v. Board of Education of Topeka, Kansas*. The case went to the U.S. Supreme Court. In 1954, the Court ruled. It said that segregation in public schools was wrong. It was illegal (il-LEE-guhl). This was a big step forward. But, the battle was not over yet.

Now the Hard Part Begins

Not all schools listened to the Court's ruling. In 1957, a federal court said the schools in Little Rock, Arkansas, must desegregate (dee-SEG-rih-gate). This means they had to let African American students into white schools. Nine African American teens signed up at Little Rock Central High School. They were the "Little Rock Nine." They tried to go to school on September 4. But, the governor sent armed guards. The guards stopped the students from entering the school. This was a violation (vye-oh-LAY-shuhn) of the court's order. That means the court's order was broken. So, on September 23, U.S. President Dwight Eisenhower stepped in. He had the teens led into the school. White parents and students made trouble. So, the African American students were taken out for their safety. The next day, armed U.S. troops came. They led the "Little Rock Nine" into the building. Once inside, the students faced lots of problems.

In 1960, Ruby Bridges started first grade. She was six years old. She went to an all-white school. Ruby was an African American. It was in New Orleans. Parents removed their children from her class. For a whole year, Ruby was in a class alone. People stood outside the school for most of the year. They shouted and carried signs.

101

Peaceful Protests Change Things

In the South, African Americans had to ride in the back of buses. If the bus filled up, African Americans had to stand up. They had to give their seats to white riders. It was a law. One day, Rosa Parks, an African American, said no. She did not give up her seat to a white man. The police arrested Rosa Parks. They put her in jail. Jo Ann Robinson, a local civil rights leader, heard about it. She made flyers. The flyers said to boycott the buses. This meant African Americans should not get on a bus. Jo Ann Robinson thought it would last one day. It lasted a year! Not one African American set foot on a bus. They rode bikes. They walked. They hoped that if they stood together, it would change the law. It worked! Then, African Americans sat wherever they liked on buses. They no longer had to give up their seats. They did not have to use fists or threats. They did not even have to act angry.

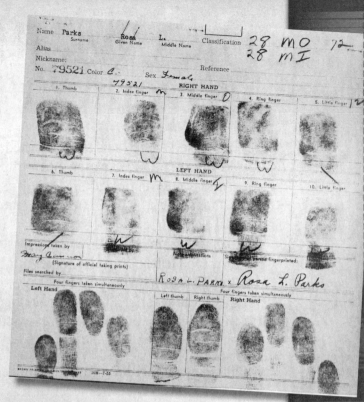

There were "white-only" lunch counters in the South. One day, four young African American men defied (DEE-fyd) this law. This means that they broke the law. They sat and ordered food at one of these "white-only" counters. The owner did not serve them. But the men did not leave. They did not get mad. They did not yell or make threats. They just sat. This was the first sit-in. More students joined them the next day. The sit-in went on for six months. As one group was arrested, another group would take its seats. At last, on July 25, 1960, things changed. The lunch counter was opened to African Americans. People held sit-ins throughout the South. Soon, all lunch counters were open to African Americans and whites.

Civil Rights Today

Many minorities (muh-NAWR-uh-teez) are still poor. A minority is a person who is part of a small group in a society. African Americans are minorities. American Indians, Latinos, and Hispanics are also minorities. Activists (ak-TUH-vistz) are people who want to make things better. Activists work to be sure that minority children get health care. They work for decent housing and good jobs. A lot of progress has been made. There is still a long way to go.

Comprehension Question

Why was Ruby Bridges in class alone the first year?

102

The Civil Rights Movement

Imagine a law that keeps you from drinking at some water fountains. Imagine restaurants that will not serve you food or drinks. Imagine on a bus, you cannot sit where you want. Why? All of this is due to your skin color. This is called segregation (seg-rih-GAY-shuhn). It is how things used to be for African Americans in parts of the United States. Segregation was very bad for those in the South. Then, some brave people decided it was time for a change. They began the Civil Rights Movement. Things started to get better.

Oliver Brown wanted his daughter to go to school. He wanted her to go to the school closest to their home. But, she was an African American. The nearby school was just for white children. The National Association for the Advancement of Colored People (NAACP) offered to help. It sued to get the girl into the white school. The lawsuit was *Brown v. Board of Education of Topeka, Kansas*. It went to the U.S. Supreme Court. In 1954, the Court said that segregation in public schools was wrong. In fact, it was illegal (il-LEE-guhl). It was a big step forward. But, the battle was not over yet.

Now the Hard Part Begins

Schools were slow to obey the Court's ruling. In 1957, a federal court told the Little Rock, Arkansas, schools to desegregate (dee-SEG-rih-gate). Nine African American students signed up at Little Rock Central High School. They tried to start school on September 4. The governor sent armed guards. The guards broke the court order and stopped the students. This was a violation (vye-oh-LAY-shuhn) of the court's order. So, on September 23, U.S. President Dwight Eisenhower stepped in. He had the "Little Rock Nine" walked into the school. But, white parents and students caused problems. So, the nine students were removed from school for their own safety. The next day, armed U.S. soldiers came. They led the students into the building. Once inside, the students faced name-calling, beatings, and threats.

In 1960, six-year-old Ruby Bridges started first grade. She entered an all-white school in New Orleans, even though she was African American. Angry parents removed their children from her class. For a whole year, Ruby was in a class all by herself. For most of the year, protesters stood outside the school. They carried signs and shouted.

Peaceful Protests Change Things

In the South, African Americans had to ride in the back of the bus. If the bus filled up, African Americans had to stand up to give their seats to white riders. It was a law. One day, Rosa Parks, an African American, would not give up her seat to a white man. The police arrested Rosa Parks. They put her in jail. Jo Ann Robinson, a local civil rights leader, heard about it. She sent out flyers. These flyers told African Americans not to ride the buses. Jo Ann Robinson said this boycott would last one day. Instead it lasted a year! Not one African American would set foot on a bus. They rode bikes. They walked. They would not get on a bus. They knew that they had to stand together to change the law. It worked! In the end, African Americans could sit wherever they liked on buses. They no longer had to give up their seats. People saw that nonviolent resistance could bring about change. Nonviolent resistance meant that they did not have to use fists or threats. They did not even have to act angry.

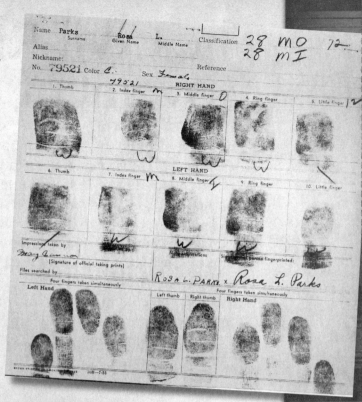

There were "white-only" lunch counters in the South. One day, four young African American men defied (DEE-fyd) the rules. They sat and ordered food at a "white-only" counter. The owner did not serve them. But the men did not leave. They were not violent. They acted with respect. This was the first sit-in. Other students joined them the next day. The sit-in went on for six months. As one group was arrested, another group would take its seats. At last, on July 25, 1960, the lunch counter was desegregated. People held sit-ins throughout the South. Soon, all lunch counters were open to African Americans and whites.

Civil Rights Today

Many minorities (muh-NAWR-uh-teez) are still poor. A minority is a person who is a member of a small group in a society. African Americans are minorities. American Indians, Latinos, and Hispanics are also minorities. Activists (ak-TUH-vistz) work to be sure that minority children get health care. They work for affordable housing and good jobs. Much progress has been made. There is still a long way to go.

Comprehension Question

What happened when Ruby Bridges started first grade?

#50084— *Leveled Texts: The 20th Century*

© *Shell Education*

The Civil Rights Movement

Imagine laws that keep you from drinking at some water fountains. Restaurants that will not serve you. Bus drivers who will not let you sit where you want on buses. All of this is happening because of your skin color. This is called segregation (seg-rih-GAY-shuhn). It is how things used to be for African Americans in parts of the United States. It was very hard for those living in the South. Then, some brave people decided it was time for a change. They began the Civil Rights Movement. Things started to improve.

Oliver Brown wanted his daughter to go to school. He wanted to send her to the one closest to their home. However, she was an African American. The nearby school was only for white children. The National Association for the Advancement of Colored People (NAACP) offered to help. It sued to get the child enrolled in the white school. The lawsuit was *Brown v. Board of Education of Topeka, Kansas*. It went to the U.S. Supreme Court in 1954. The Court said that segregation in public schools was wrong. In fact, it was illegal (il-LEE-guhl). It was a huge victory. But, the battle was far from over.

Now the Hard Part Begins

Schools were slow to obey the Supreme Court's ruling. In 1957, a federal court ordered Little Rock, Arkansas, to desegregate (dee-SEG-rih-gate) its schools. Nine African American students registered at Little Rock Central High School. They tried to start on September 4. The Arkansas governor sent armed guards to keep them out. This was a violation (vye-oh-LAY-shuhn) of the court's order. So, on September 23, U.S. President Dwight Eisenhower stepped in. He had the "Little Rock Nine" escorted into the school. However, parents and students caused problems. So, the African American students were removed for their own safety. The next day, armed U.S. soldiers arrived. They led the students into the building. Once inside, the students faced name-calling, beatings, and threats.

In 1960, six-year-old Ruby Bridges started first grade at an all-white school in New Orleans. Angry parents removed their children from Ruby's classroom. For a whole year, Ruby was in a class all by herself. For most of the year, protesters stood outside the school.

© Shell Education

#50084— Leveled Texts: The 20th Century

Peaceful Protests Change Things

In the South, African Americans had to ride in the rear of public buses. If the bus filled up, African Americans had to stand up to give their seats to white riders. One day, Rosa Parks, an African American, refused to give up her seat to a white man. The police arrested Parks. They put her in jail. Jo Ann Robinson, a local civil rights leader, sent out flyers. These flyers told African Americans not to ride the city buses. Robinson thought this boycott would last one day. Instead, it lasted a year. During that time not a single African American got on a bus. They realized that it would take all of them acting together to overturn the law. The boycott worked! In the end, African Americans could sit wherever they liked on buses, and they no longer had to give up their seats. People saw that they could use nonviolent resistance to bring about change.

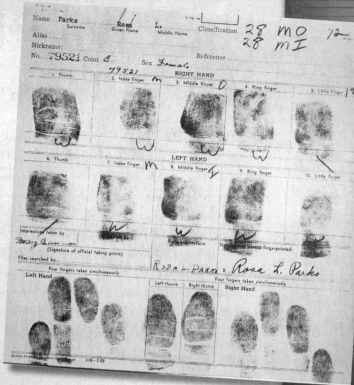

There were "white-only" lunch counters throughout the South. But one day, four young African American men defied (DEE-fyd) the rules at a Woolworth's department store. They sat and ordered food at a "white-only" lunch counter. The waitress refused to serve them, but the men did not leave. They were not violent, and they acted with respect. This was the first sit-in. Other students joined them the next day and every day for the next six months. As one group was arrested, another group would take its seats. Finally, on July 25, 1960, the lunch counter was desegregated. People staged peaceful sit-ins at segregated lunch counters throughout the South.

Civil Rights Today

Many minorities (muh-NAWR-uh-teez) still live in poverty. A minority is a person who is a member of a small group in a society. African Americans are minorities, as are American Indians, Latinos, and Hispanics. Activists (ak-TUH-vistz) work to be sure that minority children receive good health care and educational opportunities. They strive for affordable housing and job opportunities. Much progress has been made, but there is still a long way to go.

Comprehension Question

Describe Ruby Bridges's first-grade experience.

106

© Shell Education

The Civil Rights Movement

Imagine laws that prohibit you from drinking at certain water fountains. Restaurants that will not serve you, and bus drivers who will not allow you to sit wherever you want on their buses. All of this is happening because of your skin color. This is called segregation (seg-rih-GAY-shuhn), and it is how things used to be for African Americans in parts of the United States, especially those living in the South. Then, some brave individuals decided it was time for a change. They began the Civil Rights Movement, and things started to improve.

Oliver Brown wanted his daughter to go to the school closest to their Kansas home. However, she was an African American, and the nearby school was only for white children. The National Association for the Advancement of Colored People (NAACP) saw an opportunity to challenge segregation in the courts and sued to get the child enrolled in the white school. The lawsuit was *Brown v. Board of Education of Topeka, Kansas*, and it went all the way to the U.S. Supreme Court in 1954. The Court ruled that segregation in public schools was illegal (il-LEE-guhl). It was a major victory, but the battle was far from over.

Now the Hard Part Begins

Schools were slow to obey the Supreme Court's ruling. In 1957, a federal court ordered Little Rock, Arkansas, to desegregate (dee-SEG-rih-gate) its schools. The nine African American students registered at Little Rock Central High School were supposed to start on September 4, but the Arkansas governor sent armed guards to keep them out. This was a direct violation (vye-oh-LAY-shuhn) of the court's order. So, on September 23, U.S. President Dwight Eisenhower had the "Little Rock Nine" escorted into the school. However, angry parents and students caused problems, and the nine students were removed for their own safety. The next day, armed U.S. soldiers arrived and led them into the building. Once inside, the students endured name-calling, assaults, and threats.

In 1960, six-year-old Ruby Bridges started first grade at an all-white school in New Orleans, and furious parents removed their children from Ruby's classroom. For an entire year, Ruby was in a class all by herself. For most of the year, protesters stood outside the school.

© Shell Education

#50084—Leveled Texts: The 20th Century

Peaceful Protests Change Things

In the South, African Americans had to ride in the rear of public buses. If the bus filled up, African Americans had to give up their seats to white riders. One day, Rosa Parks, an African American, refused to give up her bus seat to a white man. The police arrested Parks and put her in jail. Jo Ann Robinson, a local civil rights leader, sent out flyers urging African Americans not to ride the city buses. Robinson meant for this boycott to last one day, but instead it lasted a year. During that time, not a single African American set foot on a bus. They realized that they had to act together to overturn the law. In the end, African Americans could sit wherever they liked on buses, and they no longer had to give up their seats. People saw that they could use nonviolent resistance to make positive changes.

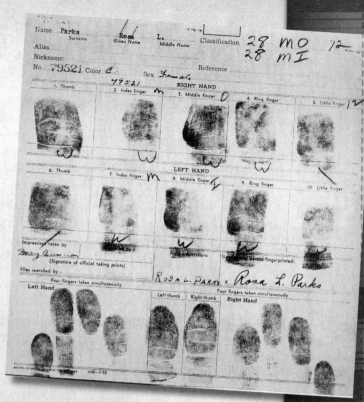

"White-only" lunch counters were a way of life in the South. But one day, four young African American men defied (DEE-fyd) those laws at a Woolworth's department store. They sat and ordered food at a "white-only" lunch counter. The waitress refused to serve them, but the men did not leave. They were not violent, and they acted with respect. This was the first sit-in. Other students joined them the next day and every day for the next six months. When one group was arrested, another group would take its place. Finally, on July 25, 1960, the lunch counter was desegregated. People staged peaceful sit-ins at segregated lunch counters throughout the South.

Civil Rights Today

Many minorities (muh-NAWR-uh-teez) still live in poverty. A minority is a person who is a member of a small group in a society. African Americans are minorities, as are American Indians, Latinos, and Hispanics. Activists (ak-TUH-vistz) work to be sure that minority children receive good health care and educational opportunities. They strive for affordable housing and job opportunities. Much progress has been made, but there is still a long way to go.

Comprehension Question

How do you think Ruby Bridges felt while sitting alone with her teacher in her classroom?

#50084— Leveled Texts: The 20th Century

© Shell Education

Dr. Martin Luther King Jr.

Dr. Martin Luther King Jr. was a preacher. In 1955, he lived in Montgomery, Alabama. That year, Rosa Parks did not give up her bus seat. She was put in jail. So, King told African Americans to stay off the buses. Not riding the buses was a boycott. It made the city leaders mad. They passed a law. It said the boycott was not legal. King did not listen to this new law. He went to jail. He was fined $500. King was shown on television. The story was printed in the newspapers. The National Association for the Advancement of Colored People (NAACP) took the case to court. The U.S. Supreme Court ruled. It said that bus segregation was wrong. It was against the law.

Dr. King was glad. He said peaceful protests would change bad laws. So, he led peaceful marches. Dr. King joined sit-ins. He did not yell or hit. King just sat in places where African Americans were not allowed. He told people not to shop at stores that were unfair to African Americans. Martin Luther King was arrested. He was put in jail many times. Still, Dr. King did not change his mind. He said violence was not the way. Then, in 1968, a man shot and killed King. King had brought the Civil Rights Movement far. Now, it had to go on without him.

March on Washington

African Americans and whites both wanted the same things. They wanted jobs, homes, and a good life. They would stand together. Asa Philip Randolph was a union leader. He set up a march. The march was in 1963. It took place on a hot day. About 250,000 people came. They marched in Washington, D.C. King gave the last speech that day. He said that he had a dream. He dreamed of the day when his "children would not be judged by the color of their skin, but by the content of their character." King's words moved all who heard him. He gave his speech in a special spot. He spoke in front of Abraham Lincoln's statue. President Lincoln had freed the slaves in the South. Lincoln had done this 100 years before.

The peaceful march changed how the public felt. The Civil Rights Movement had the support of many whites.

109

King Clashes with Some People

Some African Americans did not like King's ideas. One was Malcolm X. He said that King's nonviolence was wrong. It would not work. He told African Americans to fight for more rights. Malcolm X wanted African Americans and whites to stay apart. People who wanted fast change sided with him. He took a strong stand. It gave hope and pride to some African Americans. Later Malcolm X changed his mind. He said that African Americans and whites should work together. At that point, he was killed.

One group did not agree with King. It was the Black Panther Party for Self-Defense. The group members carried guns. King said they were wrong. He said that black people thinking they were more powerful than others was bad. It was just as bad as white people thinking they were more powerful. He said that no race was better than another.

Taking Action

Many people took part in the Civil Rights Movement. White college students left the North. They spent the summer of 1964 in Mississippi. These white college students signed up African Americans to vote. They taught children how to read and do math. They helped those who needed health or legal aid. Then, three of these civil rights activists (ak-TUH-vistz) were killed. Activists are people who fight for what they believe in. Their bodies were found months later. Helping others had cost them their lives. The nation was angered by their deaths.

In 1965, another kind of violence upset the public. In Los Angeles, a riot broke out. First, a white policeman questioned two African American brothers. A crowd gathered. More police officers came. A fight broke out. The two African American men and their mother were arrested. This started the riot. Angry African Americans smashed and burned homes and businesses. The riot lasted six days. More riots took place in other cities. These riots hurt support for the Civil Rights Movement because they were not peaceful.

Comprehension Question

Why did Dr. King lead marches?

#50084—Leveled Texts: The 20th Century

© Shell Education

Dr. Martin Luther King Jr.

Dr. Martin Luther King Jr. was a preacher. In 1955, he lived in Montgomery, Alabama. That year, Rosa Parks was put in jail when she would not give up her bus seat. King told African Americans to boycott, or stay off, the buses. This made the city leaders mad. The city leaders passed a new law. It made the boycott illegal. King went to jail for violating this new law. He was fined $500. The media (MEE-dee-uh) printed the story in the newspapers. It showed King on television. The National Association for the Advancement of Colored People (NAACP) brought the case to court. The U.S. Supreme Court ruled that bus segregation was wrong. It was not legal.

Dr. King said that peaceful protests would change unreasonable laws. He led marches. King joined peaceful sit-ins. He gave speeches. He said to boycott stores that were not fair to African Americans. Dr. King was arrested and thrown in jail many times. Still, King did not change his mind. He said violence was not the answer. Then, in 1968, a man shot and killed King. King had brought the Civil Rights Movement a long way. Now, it had to go on without him.

March on Washington

African Americans and whites both wanted the same things. They wanted jobs and homes and a good life. They could stand together. Asa Philip Randolph was a labor leader. He planned a march. In 1963, on a hot August day, 250,000 people gathered. They marched in Washington, D.C. Whites and African Americans marched. King gave the final speech that day. He said that he had a dream. He dreamed of the day when his "children would not be judged by the color of their skin, but by the content of their character." King's words moved all who heard him. He gave his speech in a special spot. He spoke in front of Abraham Lincoln's statue. President Lincoln had freed the slaves in the South. Lincoln had done this 100 years earlier.

The peaceful march changed how the public felt. The Civil Rights Movement gained the support of many white people.

© Shell Education

#50084—Leveled Texts: The 20th Century

King Clashes with Some People

Some African Americans did not like King's ideas. One man who felt this way was Malcolm X. He said that King's nonviolence would not work. Malcolm X urged African Americans to fight for more rights. Unlike King, Malcolm X wanted African Americans and whites to stay apart. People who were for fast change sided with Malcolm X. He took a strong stand. It gave hope and pride to some African Americans. Later, he changed his views. He said that African Americans and whites should work together. At that point, he was killed.

Other African Americans did not agree with King. One group was the Black Panther Party for Self-Defense. They carried guns. King said they were wrong. He said that black supremacy (suh-PREM-uh-see) was just as bad as white supremacy. He stressed that no race should be supreme, or better than another.

Taking Action

Many people played a role in the Civil Rights Movement. In 1964, white college students left the North. They spent the summer in Mississippi. They registered African American voters. They taught children how to read and do math. They helped those who needed health or legal aid. Then, three of these civil rights activists (ak-TUH-vistz), or workers, vanished. Their bodies were found months later. Helping others had cost them their lives. The public was angered by their deaths.

In 1965, another kind of violence upset the nation. In Los Angeles, a riot broke out. First, a white policeman questioned two African American brothers. As they spoke, a crowd gathered. More police officers arrived. A fight broke out. The two African American men and their mother were arrested. This started the riot. Angry African Americans smashed and burned homes and businesses. The riot lasted six days. More riots took place in other cities. These riots hurt public support for the peaceful Civil Rights Movement.

Comprehension Question

What did Dr. King believe peaceful protests would do?

#50084— *Leveled Texts: The 20th Century*

© Shell Education

Dr. Martin Luther King Jr.

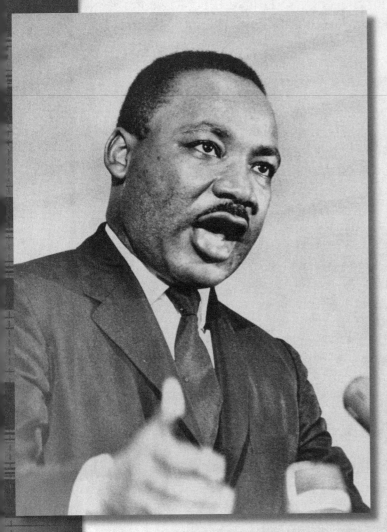

In 1955, Dr. Martin Luther King Jr. was a preacher in Montgomery, Alabama. When Rosa Parks was arrested for refusing to give up her seat on the bus, King told African Americans to stay off the buses. This made the city leaders mad, and they outlawed the boycott. They sent King to jail and fined him $500 for violating this new law. The media (MEE-dee-uh) printed the story in newspapers and showed King on television. Lawyers for the National Association for the Advancement of Colored People (NAACP) brought the case to court. The U.S. Supreme Court ruled that bus segregation was not legal.

King believed that peaceful protests would change unreasonable laws. He led marches. He participated in sit-ins. He gave fiery speeches and said to boycott stores that treated African Americans unfairly. He was arrested and thrown in jail many times. Still, King never changed his mind. Until the day he was assassinated in 1968, he said violence was not the answer. King had brought the Civil Rights Movement a long way. Now, it had to go forward without him.

March on Washington

The nation needed to see that African Americans and whites were people who wanted the same things: good jobs, homes, and happiness. So, Asa Philip Randolph, a labor-union leader, planned a march. In 1963, on a hot August day, a quarter of a million people gathered in Washington, D.C., to march for equality and jobs. King gave the final speech of the day. He said that he dreamed of the day when his "children would not be judged by the color of their skin, but by the content of their character." King's words moved all who heard him.

It was fitting that he gave this speech in front of Abraham Lincoln's statue. One hundred years earlier, Lincoln had freed the slaves in the South. This peaceful march changed how the public felt about the Civil Rights Movement. The Movement gained the support of many white people.

© Shell Education #50084— Leveled Texts: The 20th Century

King Clashes with Some People

There were some African Americans who did not like King's ideas. One of them was Malcolm X. He said that King's idea of nonviolence wouldn't work and urged African Americans to fight for their rights. Unlike King, Malcolm X wanted the races to stay apart. People who were impatient for change sided with Malcolm X. His strong stance gave hope and pride to some African Americans. Later, he changed his views. He said that African Americans and whites should work together. At that point, he, too, was assassinated.

Other African Americans disagreed with King. One group was the Black Panther Party for Self-Defense. They carried weapons. King tried to convince others that black supremacy (suh-PREM-uh-see) was just as bad as white supremacy. He stressed that no race could be supreme, or better than another.

Taking Action

Many people played a role in the Civil Rights Movement. In 1964, white college students left the North. They spent the summer in Mississippi. While there, they registered African American voters. They taught children how to read and do math. They helped those who needed medical aid or legal help. Then, three of these civil rights activists (ak-TUH-vistz) disappeared. Their bodies were found months later. Helping others had cost them their lives. The public was outraged by their deaths.

Then, in 1965, another kind of violence upset the nation. In Los Angeles, a riot broke out. First, a white policeman pulled over two African American brothers. As the officer questioned the young men, a crowd gathered. Then, more police officers arrived. A fight broke out. The two men and their mother were arrested. This sparked the riot. Frustrated African Americans smashed and burned homes and businesses. After six days of violence, the riot ended. Other riots took place all over America. These riots hurt public support for the Civil Rights Movement.

Comprehension Question

Explain in detail how King's peaceful protests changed unreasonable laws.

#50084— *Leveled Texts: The 20th Century*

© Shell Education

Dr. Martin Luther King Jr.

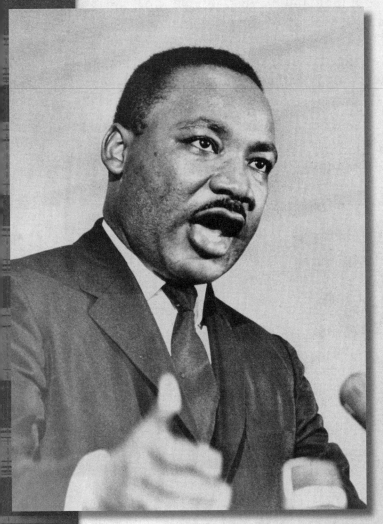

In 1955, Dr. Martin Luther King Jr. was a minister in Montgomery, Alabama. When Rosa Parks was arrested for refusing to give up her bus seat, King encouraged African Americans to stay off the buses. This infuriated city officials, and they outlawed the boycott. Then, they imprisoned King and fined him $500 for violating this new law. The media (MEE-dee-uh) showed King on television and printed the story in newspapers. Lawyers for the National Association for the Advancement of Colored People (NAACP) brought the case to court. The U.S. Supreme Court ruled that bus segregation was illegal.

King believed that peaceful protests would change unreasonable laws, so he led marches and participated in sit-ins. He gave fiery speeches and urged people to boycott stores that treated African Americans unfairly. Although he was repeatedly arrested and thrown in prison, King never changed his opinion. Until the day he was assassinated in 1968, he said violence was not the answer. King had brought the Civil Rights Movement a long way. Now, it had to go forward without him.

March on Washington

The nation needed to see that African Americans and whites could stand together. So, Asa Philip Randolph, a labor-union leader, planned a march in 1963. On a hot August day, a quarter of a million people gathered in Washington, D.C., to march for equality in the workplace. King delivered the final speech of the day. He said that he dreamed of the day when his "children would not be judged by the color of their skin, but by the content of their character." King's words moved all who heard him.

He gave this speech in front of the Lincoln Memorial. One hundred years earlier, Abraham Lincoln had freed the slaves in the South. This peaceful march changed how the nation felt about the Civil Rights Movement, and the Movement gained support from many white people.

115

King Clashes with Some People

There were some African Americans who disliked King's ideas. One of them was Malcolm X who said that King's idea of nonviolence would not work and urged African Americans to fight for equality. Also, unlike King, Malcolm X wanted the races to stay separate. People who were impatient for change sided with Malcolm X, and his strong stance gave hope and pride to some African Americans. When he changed his views and decided that African Americans and whites should work together, he was assassinated.

Other African Americans were against King's ideas, too. One group was the Black Panther Party for Self-Defense, and they carried weapons. This upset King, and he tried to convince them that black supremacy (suh-PREM-uh-see) was just as bad as white supremacy. He stressed that no race could be supreme, or better than another.

Taking Action

Many people played a role in the Civil Rights Movement. In 1964, white college students left the North to spend the summer in Mississippi. While there, they registered African American voters and taught the children how to read and do math. They helped those who needed medical aid or legal help. Three of these civil rights activists (ak-TUH-vistz) disappeared, and their bodies were found months later. It had cost them their lives to help others. The public was outraged by their murders.

Then, in 1965, another type of violence outraged the nation. In Los Angeles, a riot occurred in the African American community. It began when a white policeman pulled over two African American brothers. As the officer questioned the young men, a crowd gathered. Then, more police officers arrived. A fight broke out, and the two men and their mother were arrested. This sparked the riot. Frustrated African Americans smashed and burned homes and businesses in their community. After six days of violence, the riot ended, but other riots took place in many American cities. These riots hurt public support for the Civil Rights Movement.

Comprehension Question

Why do you think King never changed his mind about peace protests being the right way to fight injustice? Do you agree or disagree? Why?

#50084— Leveled Texts: The 20th Century

© Shell Education

The Cold War

A cold war is a war without battles. Instead, cold wars are fought with words and threats. The Cold War went on between two nations. The two nations were the United States of America and the Soviet Union. Both had such strong armies that the world called them superpowers. These nations did not trust each other. Each nation felt that the other wanted to ruin its way of life. Why? The Soviet Union had a totalitarian (toh-tah-luh-TAIR-ee-uhn) government. That means the leaders had total control. The United States has a democracy (dih-MAH-kruh-see). That means the people run the government. They chose the leaders.

The nations had different economies (eh-kon-OH-meez), too. The Soviets had communism (KAHM-yuh-nih-zuhm). This means that all land and jobs are shared. No one has more than another. A doctor earns the same as a cook. The United States has capitalism (KAP-uh-tuhl-iz-uhm). This means that people can own businesses. They earn profits. People make choices about jobs. They make choices about owning land. Some people are rich while others are poor.

The Korean War

World War II ended. Korea (kuh-REE-uh) was split in two. The plan was to put the nation back together. Then, the people would vote for new leaders. But this did not happen. The United States backed South Korea. South Korea wanted a capitalist country. The Soviets backed the North. The North had a Communist leader. Fighting broke out in Korea. On June 25, 1950, North Korea invaded South Korea.

The North had tanks and guns. They came from the Soviets. China secretly helped the North, too. The United States rushed in. It helped the South. The fighting went back and forth, but no one won. On July 27, 1953, an armistice (ARE-muhs-tuhs) was signed. An armistice is a treaty. It ended the war. Korea stayed split into two countries. It was the first time the United States did not win a war that it fought.

117

#50084—Leveled Texts: The 20th Century

The Arms Race and the Cuban Missile Crisis

The United States tested the first hydrogen bomb. This was in 1952. Within a year, the Soviets also had these bombs. They are even more deadly than atomic bombs. Leaders of both nations felt they had to be the strongest. They feared nuclear war. So, both nations began to make lots of arms, or missiles. These missiles could be sent up by pressing a button. They could fly for thousands of miles. When they fell, they would cause awful damage.

Fidel Castro (fee-DEL KAS-troh) became Cuba's ruler. He made friends with the Soviet Union. Cuba lies less than 100 miles off the coast of Florida. The Soviet leader was Nikita Khrushchev (nih-KEY-tah KROOSH-chev). He thought U.S. President John F. Kennedy was weak. In October 1962, Khrushchev set up nuclear missiles in Cuba. He aimed them at U.S. cities. Soviet ships carrying more missiles sat in the water off the coast of the United States. President Kennedy set up a naval blockade. A blockade meant United States ships blocked the Soviet ships' paths. It kept them from going forward. President Kennedy told the ships to turn back. He said all the missiles had to be removed from Cuba. Khrushchev wanted U.S. missiles taken out of Turkey. After 13 days, the men agreed. Both removed their missiles. This prevented a nuclear war.

The Vietnam War

In the early 1950s, Vietnam (VEE-et-nahm) was divided in two. There was North Vietnam and South Vietnam. Ho Chi Minh (HOH chee MIN) was the Communist leader in the North. The Soviets and Chinese helped him try to take over South Vietnam. In the early 1960s, the United States sent troops to Vietnam. They went to help the South fight the North. War was never declared against North Vietnam. Still, the fighting went on until 1975. That's when the last U.S. troops left Vietnam. Then, South Vietnam fell to North Vietnam. Once again, America had not won a war.

Results of the Cold War

During the Cold War, the United States and the Soviet Union built up nuclear arms. They tried to outdo each other in space. Both sides invented new things to stay in the lead. Microwave ovens and the Internet are just two inventions that came about. By 1991, the Cold War had ended.

Comprehension Question

Why did the United States and the Soviets make bombs?

118

© Shell Education

The Cold War

A cold war is a war without battles. Instead, cold wars are fought with words and threats. The Cold War began with two nations with big armies: the United States of America and the Soviet Union. The armies were so strong that the world called them superpowers. These two nations did not trust each other. Each one felt that the other wanted to destroy its way of life. The Soviets had a totalitarian (toh-tah-luh-TAIR-ee-uhn) government. This means that the leaders had total control. The United States has a democracy (dih-MAH-kruh-see). This means that the people control the government. How? They choose the leaders.

The two nations had different economies (eh-kon-OH-meez). The Soviets followed communism (KAHM-yuh-nih-zuhm). This means that all land and jobs are shared. No one has more than anyone else. A doctor does not earn more than a cook. The United States follows capitalism (KAP-uh-tuhl-iz-uhm). This means that people can own businesses and earn profits. People make choices about jobs and owning land. Some people are rich. Others are poor.

The Korean War

World War II ended. Then, Korea (kuh-REE-uh) was split in two. The plan was to rejoin the nation of Korea. Then, the people would vote for new leaders. But this did not happen. The United States backed South Korea. The United States wanted to set up a capitalist country. The Soviets backed the North. The North had a Communist leader. Fighting broke out in Korea. On June 25, 1950, North Korea invaded South Korea.

The North had tanks and guns. They came from the Soviets. China secretly decided to help the North, too. The United States rushed to help the South. The fighting went back and forth. There was no clear winner. On July 27, 1953, an armistice (ARE-muhs-tuhs) was signed. An armistice is a treaty that stops the fighting. It was the first time the United States did not win a war in which it fought.

The Arms Race and the Cuban Missile Crisis

The United States tested the first hydrogen bomb in 1952. Within a year, the Soviets also had these bombs. Hydrogen bombs are much more powerful than atomic ones. Leaders of both nations felt they had to be the strongest to prevent a nuclear war. They began a buildup of arms, or missiles. These missiles could be launched with the touch of a button. They could fly for thousands of miles. They would cause terrible destruction when they fell.

When Fidel Castro (fee-DEL KAS-troh) became the ruler of Cuba, he made friends with the Soviet Union. Cuba lies less than 100 miles south of Florida. The Soviet leader, Nikita Khrushchev (nih-KEY-tah KROOSH-chev), thought U.S. President John F. Kennedy was weak. In October 1962, Khrushchev set up nuclear missiles in Cuba. He aimed them at U.S. cities. Soviet ships carrying more missiles sat off the coast of the United States. President Kennedy set up a naval blockade. He told the Soviet ships to turn back. Kennedy demanded all the missiles be removed from Cuba, too. The Soviet leader wanted U.S. missiles removed from Turkey. After 13 days, both men agreed to remove their missiles. They avoided a nuclear war.

The Vietnam War

In the early 1950s, Vietnam (VEE-et-nahm) was split into North Vietnam and South Vietnam. Ho Chi Minh (HOH chee MIN) was the Communist leader in the North. The Soviets and Chinese helped him try to take over South Vietnam. The United States sent troops to help the South fight the North. War was never declared against North Vietnam, and yet the fighting dragged on until 1975. That's when the last U.S. troops withdrew from Vietnam. Then, South Vietnam fell to North Vietnam. Once again, America had not won a war.

Results of the Cold War

During the Cold War, both the United States and the Soviet Union built up nuclear weapons and also tried to outdo each other in outer space. The world changed as both sides invented new technologies to stay in the lead. Microwave ovens and the Internet are just two inventions that came about. By 1991, the Cold War had ended between the United States and the Soviet Union.

Comprehension Question

Why did the Soviets and the United States both feel they had to be the strongest?

120

The Cold War

The Cold War began with two nations with strong militaries: the United States of America and the Soviet Union. They were so strong that the world called them superpowers. The superpowers distrusted each other since each one felt that the other wanted to destroy its way of life. The Soviet Union had a totalitarian (toh-tah-luh-TAIR-ee-uhn) government, which means that the leaders had total control. The United States has a democracy (dih-MAH-kruh-see), which means that the citizens indirectly control the government by electing its leaders.

The two nations also had different economies (eh-kon-OH-meez). The Soviets followed communism (KAHM-yuh-nih-zuhm). This means that all land and jobs are shared and no one has more than anyone else. So, a doctor does not earn more than a cook. The United States follows capitalism (KAP-uh-tuhl-iz-uhm). This means that people can own businesses and earn profits. People make choices about jobs and owning land. The result is that some people are rich and others are poor.

The Korean War

When World War II ended, Korea (kuh-REE-uh) was split in two at the 38th parallel. This is a line of latitude. The plan was to rejoin the nation and let the people vote for new leaders, but it never happened. The United States backed the South and wanted to set up a capitalist country. The Soviets backed the North and its Communist leader. Fighting broke out. On June 25, 1950, North Korea invaded South Korea.

The North had tanks and guns from the Soviets. China secretly decided to help them, too. The United States rushed to help the South. The fighting went back and forth, and there was no clear winner. On July 27, 1953, an armistice (ARE-muhs-tuhs) was signed. The conflict ended. This was the first time the United States did not win a war in which it fought.

© Shell Education

#50084—Leveled Texts: The 20th Century

The Arms Race and the Cuban Missile Crisis

The United States tested the first hydrogen bomb in 1952. By 1953, the Soviets had also created hydrogen bombs. These bombs are more powerful than atomic bombs. Leaders of both nations felt they had to be the strongest to avoid a nuclear war. They began a buildup of missiles. These missiles could be launched with the touch of a button, fly for thousands of miles, and cause terrible destruction when they fell.

When Fidel Castro (fee-DEL KAS-troh) became the ruler of Cuba, he made friends with the Soviet Union. Cuba lies just 90 miles south of Florida. The Soviet leader, Nikita Khrushchev (nih-KEY-tah KROOSH-chev), thought U.S. President John F. Kennedy was weak, so in October 1962, he set up nuclear missiles in Cuba aimed at U.S. cities. Soviet ships carrying more missiles sat off the coast of the United States. Kennedy set up a naval blockade and told the Soviet ships to turn back. He demanded all the missiles be removed from Cuba as well. The Soviet leader wanted U.S. missiles removed from Turkey. After 13 days, both men agreed to remove their missiles, avoiding a nuclear war. The world breathed a sigh of relief.

The Vietnam War

In the early 1950s, Vietnam (VEE-et-nahm) was divided into North Vietnam and South Vietnam. The Communist leader in the north was Ho Chi Minh (HOH chee MIN). The Soviets and Chinese helped him try to take over South Vietnam. The United States sent troops to help the South fight the Communists. War was never declared against North Vietnam, and yet the conflict dragged on until 1975 when the last U.S. troops withdrew from Vietnam. Then, South Vietnam fell to North Vietnam. America had lost its second war.

Results of the Cold War

During the Cold War, both the United States and the Soviet Union built up nuclear arms and tried to outdo each other in space. The world changed as both sides invented new technologies to stay in the lead. Microwave ovens and the Internet are just two inventions that came about. By 1991, the Cold War had ended.

Comprehension Question

For what reasons did the Soviets find a way to create the hydrogen bomb?

© Shell Education

The Cold War

The Cold War began with two nations with strong militaries that the world called superpowers: the United States of America and the Soviet Union. These nations distrusted each other because each one felt that the other wanted to destroy its way of life. The Soviet Union had a totalitarian (toh-tah-luh-TAIR-ee-uhn) government, which means that the leaders were in complete control. The United States has a democracy (dih-MAH-kruh-see), which means that the citizens indirectly control the government by electing the leaders.

The two nations had different economies (eh-kon-OH-meez), too. The Soviets followed communism (KAHM-yuh-nih-zuhm) in which all the land and jobs are shared equally. A doctor does not earn more than a cook. No one has more than anyone else. The United States follows capitalism (KAP-uh-tuhl-iz-uhm), which lets people own businesses and earn profits. People make choices about doing jobs and owning land, and some people are wealthy while others are poor.

The Korean War

At the end of World War II, Korea (kuh-REE-uh) was divided in two at the 38th parallel. The plan was to rejoin the nation and let the citizens vote for new leaders, but it never happened. The United States supported the South and wanted to set up a capitalist country, while the Soviet Union backed the North and its Communist leader. Fighting broke out, and on June 25, 1950, North Korea invaded South Korea.

The North had tanks and guns from the Soviets. China secretly helped them to fight the war, too. The United States stepped in to help the South. The fighting went back and forth with no clear winner until July 27, 1953. On that date, an armistice (ARE-muhs-tuhs) was signed that stopped the fighting. It was the first time the United States was not victorious in a war it fought.

© Shell Education   #50084—Leveled Texts: The 20th Century

The Arms Race and the Cuban Missile Crisis

The United States tested the first hydrogen bomb in 1952. By 1953, the Soviets had also created these bombs, which are much more powerful than atomic bombs. Leaders of both nations felt they had to be the strongest to prevent a nuclear war, and they began a buildup of missiles. These missiles could be launched with the touch of a button. They could fly thousands of miles and cause terrible devastation when they landed.

When Fidel Castro (fee-DEL KAS-troh) became Cuba's ruler, he immediately made friends with the Soviet Union. Cuba lies just 90 miles south of Florida. The Soviet leader, Nikita Khrushchev (nih-KEY-tah KROOSH-chev), thought U.S. President John F. Kennedy was weak, so in October 1962, he set up nuclear missiles in Cuba that were aimed at U.S. cities. Soviet ships carrying more missiles sat off the coast of the United States. In response, Kennedy set up a naval blockade and demanded the Soviet ships turn around and all the missiles be removed from Cuba. The Soviet leader replied that he wanted U.S. missiles removed from Turkey. After 13 days, both men agreed to remove their missiles, thus avoiding a nuclear war, and the world breathed a sigh of relief.

The Vietnam War

In the early 1950s, Vietnam (VEE-et-nahm) was divided into North Vietnam and South Vietnam. The Communist leader in the north was Ho Chi Minh (HOH chee MIN), and the Soviets and Chinese assisted him with a fight against South Vietnam. The United States sent troops into South Vietnam to fight the Communists. Although war was never officially declared against North Vietnam, the conflict dragged on until 1975. That's when the last U.S. troops withdrew, and South Vietnam fell to North Vietnam. America had lost its second war.

Results of the Cold War

During the Cold War, both the United States and the Soviet Union built up nuclear arms and tried to outdo each other in space. The world changed as each superpower invented new technologies—such as microwave ovens and the Internet—in order to stay ahead. By 1991, the Cold War had ended.

Comprehension Question

What role did fear play in the arms race?

#50084—*Leveled Texts: The 20th Century*

© *Shell Education*

Conflicts in the Middle East

The Middle East is full of conflict. The trouble comes from three things. First, the creation of Israel (IZ-ree-uhl) upset those who already lived in the area. Second, religious extremists (ik-STREEM-istz) cause problems. Religious extremists have strong views. Some extremists think that people who do not follow their faith are their enemies. Third, the Middle East has lots of oil. Oil is worth a lot of money. Many nations want it.

The Modern Nation of Israel

The modern nation of Israel began in 1948. The United Nations (UN) set it up. The UN divided Palestine (PAL-uh-stine) into two parts. There was a Jewish part. There was a Palestinian (pal-uh-STIN-ee-uhn) part. Jewish people came. They built homes. They made farms. Ever since then, the Palestinians have fought against the Israelis (iz-RAY-leez). The Palestinians want the land back. They feel the UN took it from them. Arab (AIR-uhb) neighbors oppose Israel, too. Most Arabs are Muslim. Their faith is Islam. Most Israelis are Jewish. Their faith is Judaism (JOO-dee-izuhm).

Israel's first war was against five nations. They were Egypt, Syria (SEAR-ee-uh), Lebanon (LEB-uh-nuhn), Iraq (ih-RAWK), and Jordan. The Israeli army won. Then, in 1956, Israel fought Egypt only. Both wanted to control the Sinai Peninsula (SYE-nye puh-NIN-suh-luh). This land is between Egypt and Israel. Israel lost. In 1967, the same five nations struck Israel again. Israel won that war in six days. Then, Israel took more land.

In 1978, Egypt made peace with Israel. It was the first Arab nation to do so. But Islamic (iz-LAWM-ik) extremists did not like this. They think no Arab nation should make peace with Israel.

Revolution in Iran and the Palestinian Quest for Independence

Iran (ih-RAN) has lots of oil. Yet, its people were poor. Iran's ruler was rich. He was Shah Mohammed Reza Pahlavi (mo-HAM-muhd rih-ZAY PAH-luh-vee). In 1979, he became sick. He left Iran. The Shah went to get health care. While he was gone, Ayatollah Khomeini (eye-uh-TOLL-uh ko-MAY-nee) took over. Khomeini was

125

an Islamic extremist. Some Iranians (ih-RAY-nee-uhnz) hated the United States. Why? The United States had supported the Shah. On November 4, 1979, Islamic extremist students burst into the American embassy (EM-buh-see). Many U.S. people worked there. The students took 52 people hostage. They would not let them go. They were held for 444 days.

In the 1980s, many Palestinians lived in spots held by the Israeli army. These places were the West Bank and the Gaza Strip. In 1987, an uprising began. Palestinians shouted. They threw rocks at Israeli troops. So in 1993, the leaders of Palestine and Israel met. They made the Oslo Accords (OZ-low uh-KORDZ). This peace treaty let the Palestinians make their own rules. In return, they promised to stop attacking Israelis. But a lot of people on both sides were not happy. They did not like this pact. Some Palestinians still fight against Israel.

Black Gold

Together, Saudi Arabia (SAW-dee uh-RAY-bee-uh), Iraq, Kuwait (koo-WAYT), and Iran own more than half of Earth's oil. Other countries need it. They depend on oil. They use oil to make electric power. They need oil for gas for cars. They need oil for factories. Oil is one reason why the United States is involved with the Middle East.

In 1990, Iraq had a dictator. He was Saddam Hussein (suh-DAHM hoo-SAYN). He marched into Kuwait. He wanted its oil. U.S. President George H.W. Bush led a group of nations. They fought Hussein. In just weeks, Hussein was beaten. Then, the UN sent inspectors. They stayed in Iraq. They made sure that Hussein did not plan new attacks.

In 1998, Hussein threw out the inspectors. No one knew why he did that. But by 2003, some world leaders were afraid. They thought that Hussein was making dangerous weapons. U.S. President George W. Bush led several nations into Iraq. It looked like they would win fast again. Hussein died. But even then, the war did not end. In 2008, there were still U.S. troops in Iraq. They were fighting Islamic extremists. Iraqis are trying to form a new government. They want to live in freedom. They want to live in peace.

Comprehension Question

Why do some Palestinians fight the Israelis?

#50084— *Leveled Texts: The 20th Century*

© *Shell Education*

Conflicts in the Middle East

The Middle East is full of conflict. The trouble comes from three things. First, the creation of Israel (IZ-ree-uhl) sparked anger in those who already lived in the area. Second, religious extremists (ik-STREEM-istz) cause problems. These people have very strong views. For example, some of them think that all people not of their faith are enemies. Third, there is a lot of oil in the Middle East that is worth a lot of money.

The Modern Nation of Israel

The modern nation of Israel began in 1948. The United Nations (UN) set Israel up by dividing Palestine (PAL-uh-stine) into two parts. There was a Jewish part. There was a Palestinian (pal-uh-STIN-ee-uhn) part. Jewish people came. They set up homes and farms. Ever since then, some Palestinians have fought against the Israelis (iz-RAY-leez). They want to reclaim the land. The Palestinians feel the UN took the land from them. Arab (AIR-uhb) neighbors oppose Israel, too. Most Arabs are Muslim. Their faith is Islam. Most Israelis are Jewish. Their faith is Judaism (JOO-dee-izuhm).

Israel's first war was against Egypt, Syria (SEAR-ee-uh), Lebanon (LEB-uh-nuhn), Iraq (ih-RAWK), and Jordan. The strong Israeli army won. Then, in 1956, Israel fought Egypt only. Both wanted control of the Sinai Peninsula (SYE-nye puh-NIN-suh-luh). This land is between Egypt and Israel. Israel lost. In 1967, the five nations attacked Israel again. Israel won that war in six days. Then, Israel took over more land.

In 1978, Egypt made peace with Israel. It was the first Arab nation to make peace. But, Islamic (iz-LAWM-ik) extremists were upset. They did not want any Arab nation to make peace with Israel.

Revolution in Iran and the Palestinian Quest for Independence

Iran (ih-RAN) is rich in oil. In spite of this, its people were poor. Yet, Iran's ruler grew richer. He was Shah Mohammed Reza Pahlavi (mo-HAM-muhd rih-ZAY PAH-luh-vee). In 1979, the Shah became sick. He left Iran to get health care. While he was away, Ayatollah Khomeini (eye-uh-TOLL-uh ko-MAY-nee) took over Iran.

(127)

He was an Islamic extremist. Some Iranians (ih-RAY-nee-uhnz) hated the United States. The United States had backed the Shah. On November 4, 1979, Islamic extremist students burst into the American embassy (EM-buh-see). The students took 52 people hostage. They held them prisoner. They would not let them go for 444 days.

In the 1980s, many Palestinians lived in places controlled by the Israeli army. They lived in the West Bank and the Gaza Strip. In 1987, an uprising began. The Palestinians protested and threw rocks at Israeli troops. In 1993, the Palestinian and Israeli leaders met. They made the Oslo Accords (OZ-low uh-KORDZ). This agreement let the Palestinians make their own rules. In return, they promised to stop attacking Israelis. But, many people on both sides were not happy. They did not like this pact. Some Palestinians still fight against Israel today.

Black Gold

Together, Saudi Arabia (SAW-dee uh-RAY-bee-uh), Iraq, Kuwait (koo-WAYT), and Iran own more than half of the world's oil. Industrialized (in-DUHS-tree-uh-lized) countries depend on oil for gas and electric power. Industrialized nations have a lot of cars and factories. Oil is one reason why the United States is involved with the Middle East.

In 1990, Iraq's dictator was Saddam Hussein (suh-DAHM hoo-SAYN). He invaded Kuwait. He wanted that nation's oil. U.S. President George H.W. Bush led a group of nations. They fought Hussein. In just a few weeks, the

Iraqis were defeated. Then, the UN sent inspectors into Iraq. They stayed there. They made sure that Hussein did not plan new attacks.

In 1998, Hussein threw out the inspectors. No one knew why Hussein threw out the inspectors. But by 2003, some world leaders were worried. They thought that Hussein was making nuclear weapons. U.S. President George W. Bush led several nations into Iraq. At first, it looked like they would quickly win. But even after Hussein died, the war did not end. As of 2008, there were still U.S. troops in Iraq. They were fighting Islamic extremists. The people of Iraq are trying to form a new government. They want to live in freedom and peace.

Comprehension Question

Why were some Palestinians angry with the United Nations?

#50084—Leveled Texts: The 20th Century

© Shell Education

Conflicts in the Middle East

The Middle East is filled with conflict. It comes from three issues. First, the creation of Israel (IZ-ree-uhl) sparked conflict with those who already lived in the region. Second, religious extremists (ik-STREEM-istz) cause trouble. These people have extreme views. For example, some of them think that all people of different faiths are their enemies. Third, there is a lot of oil in the Middle East, and it's worth a fortune.

The Modern Nation of Israel

The modern nation of Israel began in 1948. The United Nations (UN) divided Palestine (PAL-uh-stine) into two parts. There was a Jewish section and a Palestinian (pal-uh-STIN-ee-uhn) section. Jewish people came to the new country and set up homes and farms. Ever since then, some Palestinians have fought against the Israelis (iz-RAY-leez) to reclaim the land they feel the UN took from them. Israel also has Arab (AIR-uhb) neighbors who oppose them. Most Israelis are Jewish and believe in Judaism (JOO-dee-izuhm). Most Arabs are Muslims who practice Islam.

Israel's first war was against Egypt, Syria (SEAR-ee-uh), Lebanon (LEB-uh-nuhn), Iraq (ih-RAWK), and Jordan. The strong Israeli army won. Then, in 1956, Israel fought Egypt for control of the Sinai Peninsula (SYE-nye puh-NIN-suh-luh). It lies between Egypt and Israel. Israel lost this war. In 1967, the same five nations attacked Israel again. Israel won that war in just six days and took control of more land.

In 1978, Egypt was the first Arab country to make peace with Israel. But, Islamic (iz-LAWM-ik) extremists were unhappy. They did not want any Arab nation to make a treaty with Israel.

Revolution in Iran and the Palestinian Quest for Independence

Iran (ih-RAN) is very rich in oil. In spite of this, its people were poor. At the same time, Iran's ruler grew richer. His name was Shah Mohammed Reza Pahlavi (mo-HAM-muhd rih-ZAY PAH-luh-vee). In 1979, the Shah had cancer and left Iran

© Shell Education #50084— Leveled Texts: The 20th Century

to get medical treatment. While he was away, Ayatollah Khomeini (eye-uh-TOLL-uh ko-MAY-nee), an Islamic extremist, took over Iran. Some Iranians (ih-RAY-nee-uhnz) hated the United States for having supported the Shah. On November 4, 1979, Islamic extremist students stormed the American embassy (EM-buh-see). The students broke in and held 52 people hostage for 444 days.

During the 1980s, many Palestinians lived in places controlled by the Israeli army. They lived in the West Bank and the Gaza Strip. In 1987, an uprising began in which the Palestinians protested and threw rocks at Israeli soldiers. In 1993, the Palestinian and Israeli leaders met and made the Oslo Accords (OZ-low uh-KORDZ). This agreement let the Palestinians make their own rules. In return, they had to stop attacking the Israelis. But, many people on both sides were unhappy with this agreement. Some Palestinians continue to fight against Israel today.

Black Gold

Together, Saudi Arabia (SAW-dee uh-RAY-bee-uh), Iraq, Kuwait (koo-WAYT), and Iran have more than half of the world's oil. Industrialized (in-DUHS-tree-uh-lized) countries depend on oil for gas and electricity. Oil is one of the reasons the United States is involved with the Middle East.

In 1990, Iraq's dictator was Saddam Hussein (suh-DAHM hoo-SAYN). He invaded Kuwait to get that nation's oil. U.S. President George H.W. Bush led a group of nations against Hussein. In just a few weeks, the Iraqis were defeated. Then, the UN sent inspectors into Hussein's country to make sure that he would not plan any new attacks.

In 1998, Hussein threw out the inspectors. No one knew exactly why he did that, but by 2003, some world leaders feared that he was making nuclear weapons. U.S. President George W. Bush led several nations in an attack on Iraq. At first, it looked like they would quickly win. But even after Hussein died, the conflict continued. As of 2008, there were U.S. soldiers fighting against Islamic extremists in Iraq. The people of Iraq are trying to form a new government and want to live in peace.

Comprehension Question

Describe how Israel came to be a country, and explain why this has created problems for some people in that region.

Conflicts in the Middle East

The Middle East is filled with conflict that stems from three major issues. First, the creation of Israel (IZ-ree-uhl) sparked conflict with those who already lived in the region. Second, religious extremists (ik-STREEM-istz) cause trouble. These people have extreme opinions. For example, some people think that all those of different faiths are their enemies. Third, there is an abundance of oil in the Middle East, and many nations want it.

The Modern Nation of Israel

The modern nation of Israel began in 1948. After World War II, the United Nations (UN) divided Palestine (PAL-uh-stine) into two sections: Jewish and Palestinian (pal-uh-STIN-ee-uhn). Jewish people came to the new country and established homes and farms. Ever since then, some Palestinians have fought against the Israelis (iz-RAY-leez) to reclaim the territory that they feel the UN unfairly took from them. Israel also has Arab (AIR-uhb) neighbors who oppose Israelis. Most Israelis are Jewish and practice Judaism (JOO-dee-izuhm). Most Arabs are Muslims who practice Islam.

Israel fought and won against an attack by the Arab nations of Egypt, Syria (SEAR-ee-uh), Lebanon (LEB-uh-nuhn), Iraq (ih-RAWK), and Jordan. Then, in 1956, Israel fought Egypt for control of the Sinai Peninsula (SYE-nye puh-NIN-suh-luh) which lies between the two nations. Israel lost this war. In 1967, the same five nations attacked Israel again. Israel won in just six days and took control of more land.

In 1978, Egypt was the first Arab country to make peace with Israel. But, Islamic (iz-LAWM-ik) extremists were unhappy because they did not want any Arab country to make treaties with Israel.

Revolution in Iran and the Palestinian Quest for Independence

Iran (ih-RAN) has a great deal of oil and thus should be rich. Despite this, its people were impoverished, while simultaneously Iran's ruler grew wealthier. His name was Shah Mohammed Reza Pahlavi (mo-HAM-muhd rih-ZAY PAH-luh-vee). The Shah had cancer in 1979, and he left Iran to get medical treatment. While he

131

was gone, Ayatollah Khomeini (eye-uh-TOLL-uh ko-MAY-nee), an Islamic extremist, seized control of Iran. Some Iranians (ih-RAY-nee-uhnz) hated the United States for having supported the Shah. On November 4, 1979, Islamic extremist students stormed the American embassy (EM-buh-see). The extremists broke in, took 52 people hostage, and held them captive for 444 days.

During the 1980s, many Palestinians lived in the West Bank and the Gaza Strip, which were controlled by the Israeli army. In 1987, an uprising began in which Palestinians protested and threw rocks at Israeli soldiers. In 1993, the Palestinian and Israeli leaders met and made the Oslo Accords (OZ-low uh-KORDZ), an agreement that allowed the Palestinians to make their own rules. In return, they committed to stop attacking Israelis. But, many people on both sides were dissatisfied with this agreement, and some Palestinians continue to fight against Israel today.

Black Gold

Together, Saudi Arabia (SAW-dee uh-RAY-bee-uh), Iraq, Kuwait (koo-WAYT), and Iran own more than half of Earth's oil. Industrialized (in-DUHS-tree-uh-lized) countries depend on oil for gas and electricity. Oil is one of the major reasons the United States is involved with the Middle East.

In 1990, Iraq's dictator, Saddam Hussein (suh-DAHM hoo-SAYN), invaded Kuwait to get that nation's oil. U.S. President George H.W. Bush led a group of nations against Hussein and defeated the Iraqis in weeks. Then, the UN sent inspectors into Hussein's country to make sure that he would not plan any new attacks.

In 1998, Hussein threw out the inspectors. No one knew exactly why he did that, but by 2003, some world leaders feared that he was making nuclear weapons. U.S. President George W. Bush led several nations in an attack on Iraq. It looked as though they would quickly win, yet even after Hussein died, the conflict continued. As of 2008, there were U.S. soldiers fighting against Islamic extremists in Iraq. The people of Iraq are trying to form a new government and want to live in freedom and peace.

Comprehension Question

Explain why some Palestinians were not satisfied with the Oslo Accords.

© Shell Education

Modern World Leaders

World leaders must take stands. They must make hard choices. Not everyone likes what they do. The leaders do not know what the future holds. Still, they must think ahead. They must guess how things will turn out. Leaders must think about their nation's actions. They must think about other nations' actions.

Anwar Sadat, Menachem Begin, and Jimmy Carter

Egypt fought in five wars against Israel (IZ-ree-uhl). These five wars took place between 1948 and 1973. In 1978, the Egyptian leader was Anwar Sadat (AHN-whar suh-DOT). He wanted peace with Israel. U.S. President Jimmy Carter asked Anwar Sadat to visit the United States. He asked an Israeli (iz-RAY-lee) leader to come, too. Prime Minister Menachem Begin (muh-NAW-kuhm BAY-ghin) joined them. Carter helped the men to talk about their problems. At last, Egypt and Israel agreed. They signed the Camp David Accords (uh-KORDZ). It was a peace treaty. But, Islamic (iz-LAWM-ik) extremists (ik-STREEM-istz) were not happy. They did not want peace with Israel. Extremists often do shocking things. A few years later, they killed Sadat.

In 1979, Islamic extremist students broke into the U.S. embassy (EM-buh-see) in Iran. They took 52 people hostage. They would not let them go. President Carter tried to free them. Nothing worked. The kidnappers did not like Carter. After 444 days, they let the people go. It was the day President Ronald Reagan took office.

Mikhail Gorbachev and Ronald Reagan

In 1985, the Soviet Union had a new leader. Mikhail Gorbachev (mick-HAIL GORE-buh-chof) wanted to change communism. He wanted businesses to compete. Many Soviet leaders did not like him. They did not want to let their people have freedoms.

Ronald Reagan was the U.S. president. He saw that Gorbachev was a smart man. Both nations had spent too much money on the arms race. The countries had made lots of weapons. Many people feared a nuclear war. Gorbachev and Reagan chose to stop the arms race. They ended the Cold War. It was good for the whole world.

133

Yasir Arafat and Yitzhak Rabin

Yasir Arafat (YAH-sir AIR-uh-fat) led the Palestinian (pal-uh-STIN-ee-uhn) Liberation Organization (PLO). The PLO led attacks against Israel. They attacked again and again. Many Israelis died. As a result, the Israelis treated the Palestinians poorly.

In 1992, the Israeli prime minister was Yitzhak Rabin (YIT-sock rah-BEAN). He wanted peace. In 1993, Arafat and Rabin met. They made an agreement. It was called the Oslo Accords. But, not everyone liked it. Some Palestinians kept up the strikes against Israel. Some Israelis said the Palestinians must pay for the attacks. A Jewish extremist killed Rabin in 1995. Rabin had taken the first steps toward peace. For that, he was killed.

Saddam Hussein Against the World

Saddam Hussein (suh-DAHM hoo-SAYN) ruled Iraq (ih-RAWK). In 1990, he marched into Kuwait (koo-WAYT). He did this after the United Nations (UN) told him not to do so. Kuwait borders Iraq. Kuwait is small. But it has just as much oil as Iraq. U.S. President George H. W. Bush led a group of nations. They fought against Hussein. This was the Persian Gulf War. In just weeks, the Iraqis were beaten. Then, the UN sent inspectors. They stayed in Iraq. They made sure that Hussein did not plan more attacks. But in 1998, he threw out the inspectors. No one knew why. What was he trying to hide? Some world leaders feared Hussein was hiding nuclear weapons.

No one wanted this unfriendly man to own such weapons. So in 2003, U.S. President George W. Bush led other nations. They went into Iraq. Hussein was hanged to death. Yet, the war went on. In 2008, U.S. troops were still there. They were fighting Islamic insurgents (in-SURG-uhntz). These people want to keep Iraq from having a new government.

Comprehension Question

Name one reason Saddam Hussein marched into Kuwait?.

#50084 — Leveled Texts: The 20th Century

© Shell Education

Modern World Leaders

World leaders must take stands. They must make hard choices. Not everyone likes what they do. The leaders do not know what the future will bring. Still, they must think ahead. Leaders must predict how things will turn out based on their own and others' actions.

Anwar Sadat, Menachem Begin, and Jimmy Carter

Egypt fought in five wars against Israel (IZ-ree-uhl). These wars took place between 1948 and 1973. In 1978, the Egyptian leader was Anwar Sadat (AHN-whar suh-DOT). He wanted to make peace with Israel. U.S. President Jimmy Carter invited Sadat to the United States. He asked the Israeli (iz-RAY-lee) prime minister, Menachem Begin (muh-NAW-kuhm BAY-ghin), to come, too. Carter went back and forth between the men with notes. At last, they agreed. They signed the Camp David Accords

(uh-KORDZ). It was a peace treaty. The two leaders won the Nobel Peace Prize for making this treaty. This prize is given to people who work for peace. But, Islamic (iz-LAWM-ik) extremists (ik-STREEM-istz) were not happy. They did not want peace with Israel. Extremists often do shocking things. A few years later, they killed Sadat.

Jimmy Carter was president during the Iran hostage crisis. Islamic extremist students broke into the U.S. embassy in Iran. They took 52 Americans hostage. They held them prisoner. Carter tried to get them set free. Nothing he did worked. The kidnappers did not like Carter. After 444 days, they let the hostages go. It was the day President Ronald Reagan took office.

Mikhail Gorbachev and Ronald Reagan

In 1985, the Soviet Union had a new leader. Mikhail Gorbachev (mick-HAIL GORE-buh-chof) wanted to change communism. He wanted to let businesses compete. Many Soviet leaders did not like him. They did not want to let their people have freedoms.

Ronald Reagan was the United States president. He saw that Gorbachev was a reasonable man. Both nations had spent too much money on nuclear weapons. Many people lived in fear of a nuclear war. Gorbachev and Reagan agreed to end the arms race. This ended the Cold War. It was a relief to the whole world.

135

Yasir Arafat and Yitzhak Rabin

Yasir Arafat (YAH-sir AIR-uh-fat) led the Palestinian (pal-uh-STIN-ee-uhn) Liberation Organization (PLO). The PLO led many violent attacks against Israel. As a result, the Israelis treated the Palestinians poorly.

In 1992, Israel elected Prime Minister Yitzhak Rabin (YIT-sock rah-BEAN). He had fought in the wars between Israel and its Arab (AIR-uhb) neighbors. Now, Rabin wanted to make peace. In 1993, Arafat and Rabin reached an agreement. It was called the Oslo Accords. But, not everyone liked it. Some Palestinians kept up the violence against Israelis. Some Israelis wanted the Palestinians to pay for these attacks. A Jewish extremist killed Rabin in 1995. The first steps toward peace with the Palestinians began with Prime Minister Rabin. He was killed trying to make peace between the Palestinians and Israelis. People who long for peace still honor him.

Saddam Hussein Against the World

Saddam Hussein (suh-DAHM hoo-SAYN) was the ruler of Iraq (ih-RAWK). In 1990, he marched into Kuwait (koo-WAYT). He did this after the United Nations (UN) told him not to do so. Kuwait is small. It borders Iraq. Kuwait produces just as much oil as Iraq. U.S. President George H. W. Bush led a group of nations. They went against Hussein. This was the Persian Gulf War. In just weeks, the Iraqi army was defeated. Then, the UN sent inspectors. They stayed in Iraq to make sure that Hussein did not plan more attacks. But in 1998, Hussein threw out the inspectors. No one was sure why he threw out these inspectors. Some world leaders thought that he was making nuclear weapons and did not want anyone to know about these weapons.

No one wanted such a hostile man to own such weapons. So, in 2003, U.S. President George W. Bush led other nations to attack Iraq. They went into Iraq. Hussein was hanged. Yet, the war did not end. In 2008, U.S. troops were still there. They were fighting Islamic insurgents (in-SURG-uhntz). These people want to prevent Iraq from having a new government.

Comprehension Question

Why did Saddam Hussein want to take over Kuwait?

© Shell Education

Modern World Leaders

World leaders must make hard decisions. Sometimes, they take unpopular stands. They never know for sure what the future will bring. Still, they must make predictions. Leaders must think about what will happen based on their own and others' actions.

Anwar Sadat, Menchem Begin, and Jimmy Carter

Egypt fought in five wars against Israel (IZ-ree-uhl). These wars took place between 1948 and 1973. In 1978, the Egyptian president was Anwar Sadat (AHN-whar suh-DOT). He decided to make peace with Israel. U.S. President Jimmy Carter invited Sadat and Menachem Begin (muh-NAW-kuhm BAY-ghin), the Israeli (iz-RAY-lee) prime minister, to the United States. At first, the leaders would not speak to each other. Carter had to go back and forth between them with messages. At last, they agreed to the Camp David Accords (uh-KORDZ). The two leaders received the Nobel Peace Prize for making this treaty. Unfortunately, not everyone was happy with it. A few years later, Islamic (iz-LAWM-ik) extremists (ik-STREEM-istz) assassinated Sadat.

Jimmy Carter was president during the Iran hostage crisis, too. Islamic extremists broke into the U.S. embassy (EM-buh-see) in Iran and took 52 Americans hostage. Carter tried to get them set free. Nothing he did worked. The kidnappers did not like him. They released the hostages when President Ronald Reagan took office.

Mikhail Gorbachev and Ronald Reagan

In 1985, a new leader rose to power in the Soviet Union. Mikhail Gorbachev (mick-HAIL GORE-buh-chof) wanted to change communism so that businesses could compete. Many Soviet officials did not like him. They did not want to let their people have freedoms.

Ronald Reagan was the United States president. He saw that Gorbachev was a reasonable man. Both nations had spent too much on nuclear weapons. Many people lived in fear of a nuclear war. Gorbachev and Reagan agreed to end the arms race. This ended the Cold War and was a victory for the whole world.

© Shell Education

#50084—Leveled Texts: The 20th Century

Yasir Arafat and Yitzhak Rabin

Yasir Arafat (YAH-sir AIR-uh-fat) led the Palestinian (pal-uh-STIN-ee-uhn) Liberation Organization, or PLO. The PLO led many violent attacks against Israel. As a result, the Israelis treated the Palestinians poorly.

In 1992, Israel elected Prime Minister Yitzhak Rabin (YIT-sock rah-BEAN). He had fought in many of the wars between Israel and its Arab (AIR-uhb) neighbors. Now, he wanted to bring peace to the region. In 1993, Arafat and Rabin reached an agreement. It was called the Oslo Accords. But, not everyone liked it. Some Palestinians continued the violence against the Israelis. Some Israelis wanted the Palestinians to pay for these attacks. A Jewish extremist assassinated Rabin in 1995. The first steps toward peace with the Palestinians began with Prime Minister Rabin. People who long for peace in the Middle East still honor him.

Saddam Hussein Against the World

Saddam Hussein (suh-DAHM hoo-SAYN) was the ruler of Iraq (ih-RAWK). In 1990, he invaded the tiny country of Kuwait (koo-WAYT). He did this after the United Nations (UN) warned him not to do so. Kuwait borders Iraq and produces just as much oil as Iraq. U.S. President George H. W. Bush led a group of nations against Hussein. This was the Persian Gulf War. In just weeks, the Iraqi army was defeated. Then, the UN sent inspectors to stay in Iraq to make sure that Hussein did not plan more attacks. But in 1998, Hussein threw out the UN inspectors. No one was certain why. Some world leaders suspected that he was making nuclear weapons.

No one wanted such an aggressive man to own such weapons. So, in 2003, U.S. President George W. Bush led other nations in an attack on Iraq. Hussein was hanged. Yet, the war continued. As of 2008, U.S. troops were still there. They were fighting Islamic insurgents (in-SURG-uhntz) who want to prevent Iraq from forming a new government.

Comprehension Question

Describe the reasons for the Persian Gulf War.

138

© Shell Education

Modern World Leaders

World leaders must make tough decisions. Sometimes, they take unpopular stands. They never know, for sure, what the future will bring. Still, they must make predictions about what will happen based on their own and others' actions.

Anwar Sadat, Menachem Begin, and Jimmy Carter

Egypt fought in five wars against Israel (IZ-ree-uhl) between 1948 and 1973. In 1978, the Egyptian president, Anwar Sadat (AHN-whar suh-DOT), decided to make peace with Israel. U.S. President Jimmy Carter invited Sadat and Menachem Begin (muh-NAW-kuhm BAY-ghin), the Israeli (iz-RAY-lee) prime minister, to come to the United States. At first, the leaders would not speak to each other, so Carter had to go back and forth between them with messages. At last, they agreed to the Camp David Accords (uh-KORDZ). The two leaders received the Nobel Peace Prize for this treaty.

Unfortunately, not everyone was happy with it. A few years later, Islamic (iz-LAWM-ik) extremists (ik-STREEM-istz) assassinated Sadat.

Jimmy Carter was president during the Iran hostage crisis, too. After Islamic extremists broke into the U.S. embassy (EM-buh-see) in Iran and took 52 Americans hostage, he tried to get them set free. Nothing he did worked because the kidnappers did not like him. They released the hostages the day that President Ronald Reagan took office.

Mikhail Gorbachev and Ronald Reagan

In 1985, a new leader came to power in the Soviet Union. Mikhail Gorbachev (mick-HAIL GORE-buh-chof) wanted to change communism so that businesses could compete. Many Soviet officials did not like him and were afraid to let their citizens have freedoms.

Ronald Reagan, the United States president, saw that Gorbachev was a reasonable man. Both nations had spent too much money on nuclear weapons, and many people lived in fear of a nuclear war. Gorbachev and Reagan agreed to end the arms race. This brought about the end of the Cold War and was a victory for the entire world.

© Shell Education

Yasir Arafat and Yitzhak Rabin

Yasir Arafat (YAH-sir AIR-uh-fat) was the leader of the Palestinian (pal-uh-STIN-ee-uhn) Liberation Organization, or PLO. The PLO led many violent attacks against Israel, which resulted in the Israelis treating the Palestinians poorly.

In 1992, Israel elected Prime Minister Yitzhak Rabin (YIT-sock rah-BEAN). Although he had fought in many of the wars between Israel and its Arab (AIR-uhb) neighbors, he wanted to bring peace to the region. In 1993, Arafat and Rabin reached an agreement called the Oslo Accords. But, not everyone agreed with it. Some Palestinians continued the violence against Israelis, and some Israelis wanted the Palestinians to pay for the attacks on them. A Jewish extremist assassinated Rabin in 1995. Since the first steps toward peace with the Palestinians began with Prime Minister Rabin, people who long for peace in the Middle East still honor him.

Saddam Hussein Against the World

Saddam Hussein (suh-DAHM hoo-SAYN) was the ruler of Iraq (ih-RAWK). In 1990, he invaded the tiny country of Kuwait (koo-WAYT) after the United Nations (UN) warned him not to do so. Kuwait borders Iraq and produces just as much oil as Iraq. U.S. President George H. W. Bush led a group of nations against Hussein in the Persian Gulf War. In just weeks, the Iraqi army was defeated. After that, the UN sent inspectors to stay in Iraq to make sure that Hussein did not plan more attacks. But in 1998, Hussein threw out the UN inspectors, and no one was certain why. Some world leaders suspected that he was making nuclear weapons.

Nobody wanted an aggressive dictator like Hussein to have such weapons. So in 2003, U.S. President George W. Bush led other nations in an attack on Iraq. Everyone thought the war would end quickly. Hussein was hanged, but still the war dragged on. As of 2008, U.S. troops were still there, fighting Islamic insurgents (in-SURG-uhntz) who want to prevent Iraq from having a new government.

Comprehension Question

What made Kuwait a perfect target for Saddam Hussein, and why were other nations concerned about his invasion?

#50084— *Leveled Texts: The 20th Century*

© Shell Education

Resources

References Cited

August, Diane and Timothy Shanahan (Eds). (2006). *Developing literacy in second-language learners: Report of the National Literacy Panel on language-minority children and youth.* Mahwah, NJ: Lawrence Erlbaum Associates, Inc.

Marzano, Robert, Debra Pickering, and Jane Pollock. (2001). *Classroom instruction that works.* Alexandria, VA: Association for Supervision and Curriculum Development.

Tomlinson, Carol Ann. (2000). *Leadership for Differentiating Schools and Classrooms*, Alexandria, VA: Association for Supervision and Curriculum Development.

Image Sources

Page	Description	Photo Credit/Source	Filename
21, 23, 25, 27 (top)	Lincoln Cotton Mills, Evansville, Ind. Girls at weaving machine	The Library of Congress, Prints and Photographs Division. Washington, D.C. (LC-DIG-nclc-01336)	weaver.jpg
21, 23, 25, 27 (bottom)	19th-Century stock certificate	Robert O. Brown Photography/ Shutterstock, Inc. (681667)	stock.jpg
22, 24, 26, 28	*The New York World* newspaper for March 16, 1911, showing Triangle Shirtwaist Company disaster	The Library of Congress, Prints and Photographs Division. Washington, D.C. (LC-USZ62-122315)	paper,jpg
29, 31, 33, 35 (top)	Laying out plates on hot bed at a steel mill	The Library of Congress, Prints and Photographs Division. Washington, D.C. (LC-USZ62-107112)	steel.jpg
29, 31, 33, 35 (bottom)	Political cartoon of a Standard Oil tank	The Library of Congress, Prints and Photographs Division. Washington, D.C. (LC-USZC4-435)	oil.jpg
30, 32, 34, 36	Cars ready for delivery	The Library of Congress, Prints and Photographs Division. Washington, D.C. (LC-USZ62-63968)	cars.jpg
37, 39, 41, 43 (top)	Statue of Liberty	Mike Liu/Shutterstock, Inc. (2325594)	liberty.jpg
37, 39, 41, 43 (bottom)	Family working on piecework together	The Library of Congress, Prints and Photographs Division. Washington, D.C. (http://hdl.loc.gov/loc.pnp/nclc.04274)	family.jpg
38, 40, 42, 44	Tenement life	New York Public Library (732936F)	tenement.jpg
45, 47, 49, 51	Chinese workers canning salmon	The Library of Congress, Prints and Photographs Division. Washington, D.C. (LC-USZ62-95113)	canning.jpg
46, 48, 50, 52	Cartoon showing that some in Oregon were not fond of having Chinese immigrants	The Library of Congress, Prints and Photographs Division. Washington, D.C. (LC-USZC2-1213)	cartoon.jpg
53, 55, 57, 59 (top)	Swiss soldiers entrenched on the frontier (1914–1916)	The Library of Congress, Prints and Photographs Division. Washington, D.C. (LC-USZ62-114956)	trenches.jpg

© Shell Education

Resources (cont.)

Image Sources (cont.)

Page	Description	Photo Credit/Source	Filename
53, 55, 57, 59 (bottom)	R.M.S. *Lusitania*, hit by torpedoes off Kinsale Head, Ireland	The Library of Congress, Prints and Photographs Division. Washington, D.C. (LC-USZC4-13285)	ship.jpg
54, 56, 58, 60	Zimmermann telegram sent January 19, 1917	The National Archives	telegram.jpg
61, 63, 65, 67	Women suffragists picketing in front of the White House	The Library of Congress, Prints and Photographs Division. Washington, D.C. (http://teachpol.tcnj.edu/amer_pol_hist/fi/00000126.htm)	women.jpg
62, 64, 66, 68 (top)	Louis Armstrong, 1900–1971	The Library of Congress, Prints and Photographs Division. Washington, D.C. (LC-USZ62-127236)	armstrng.jpg
62, 64, 66, 68 (bottom)	Three suffragists casting votes in New York City	The Library of Congress, Prints and Photographs Division. Washington, D.C. (LC-USZ62-75334)	vote.jpg
69, 71, 73, 75	Okies on their way to California	The Library of Congress, Prints and Photographs Division. Washington, D.C. (LC-USZ62-69109)	west.jpg
70, 72, 74, 76 (top)	Franklin Delano Roosevelt making speech to crowd	The Library of Congress, Prints and Photographs Division. Washington, D.C. (LC-USZ62-99926)	fdr.jpg
70, 72, 74, 76 (bottom)	Eleanor Roosevelt talking to a woman machinist	The Library of Congress, Prints and Photographs Division. Washington, D.C. (LC-DIG-ppmsca-01946)	eleanor.jpg
77, 79, 81, 83 (top)	Adolf Hitler standing in open-air automobile	The Library of Congress, Prints and Photographs Division. Washington, D.C. (LC-USZ62-72155)	hitler.jpg
77, 79, 81, 83 (bottom)	British prisoners at Dunkerque, France, June 1940	The National Archives (http://www.archives.gov/research/ww2/photos/images/ww2-80.jpg)	soldiers.jpg
78, 80, 82, 84	German prisoners	The Library of Congress, Prints and Photographs Division. Washington, D.C. (LC-DIG-ggbain-25803)	prisoner.jpg
85, 87, 89, 91	Two LSTs on Leyte Island beach	The National Archives (http://www.archives.gov/research/ww2/photos/images/ww2-151.jpg)	arriving.jpg
86, 88, 90, 92	General panoramic view of Hiroshima after the bomb	The Library of Congress, Prints and Photographs Division. Washington, D.C. (LC-USZ62-134192)	bomb.jpg
93, 95, 97, 99 (top)	Prime Minister Winston Churchill of Great Britain	The Library of Congress, Prints and Photographs Division. Washington, D.C. (LC-USW33-019093-C)	churchil.jpg
93, 95, 97, 99 (bottom)	Adolf Hitler	Photos.com (36904666)	hitler2.jpg
94, 96, 98, 100 (top)	President Harry S. Truman delivering a speech	The Library of Congress, Prints and Photographs Division. Washington, D.C. (LC-USZ62-86087)	truman.jpg
94, 96, 98, 100 (bottom)	Hirohito being enthroned	The Library of Congress, Prints and Photographs Division. Washington, D.C. (LC-USZC2-724)	emperor.jpg
101, 103, 105, 107	Drinking fountain on the county courthouse lawn, Halifax, North Carolina	The Library of Congress, Prints and Photographs Division. Washington, D.C. (LC-DIG-ppmsc-00216)	boy.jpg

© Shell Education

Resources *(cont.)*

Image Sources *(cont.)*

Page	Description	Photo Credit/Source	Filename
102, 104, 106, 108	Rosa Parks's fingerprints	The National Archives (http://www.archives.gov/education/lessons/rosa-parks/index.html)	parks.jpg
109, 111, 113, 115	Martin Luther King Jr.	The Library of Congress, Prints and Photographs Division. Washington, D.C. (LC-USZ62-122992)	king.jpg
110, 112, 114, 116	March on Washington for Jobs and Freedom, August 28, 1963	The Library of Congress, Prints and Photographs Division. Washington, D.C. (LC-U9-10364-37)	march.jpg
117, 119, 121, 123	Mao Zedong	The Library of Congress, Prints and Photographs Division. Washington, D.C. (LC-USZC4-3345)	mao.jpg
118, 120, 122, 124 (top)	Atomic blast	The Library of Congress, Prints and Photographs Division. Washington, D.C. (LC-USZ62-66049)	bomb02.jpg
118, 120, 122, 124 (bottom)	Fidel Castro arrives in Washington, D.C., 1959	The Library of Congress, Prints and Photographs Division. Washington, D.C. (RR031900)	castro.jpg
125, 127, 129, 131	Temple of the dome, with Israeli flag on foreground	Boris Katsman/Shutterstock, Inc. (2881549)	temple.jpg
126, 128, 130, 132	Iraq oil field pump jack	Douglas Knight/Shutterstock, Inc. (2415443)	iraq.jpg
133, 135, 137, 139	President Jimmy Carter welcomes Sadat at the White House, Washington, D.C., 1980	The Library of Congress, Prints and Photographs Division. Washington, D.C. (LC-DIG-ppmsca-09815)	leaders.jpg
134, 136, 138, 140	Close-up of 100 Iraqi dinars banknote. Features Saddam Hussein.	Matt Trommer/Shutterstock, Inc. (3392035)	hussein.jpg

© *Shell Education* *#50084—Leveled Texts: The 20th Century*

Resources *(cont.)*

Contents of Teacher Resource CD

PDF Files

The full-color pdfs provided are each eight pages long and contain all four levels of a reading passage. For example, European Immigration PDF (pages 37–44) is the *european.pdf* file.

Text Files

The *Microsoft Word* documents include the text for all four levels of each reading passage. For example, European Immigration text (pages 37–44) is the *european.doc* file.

Text Title	Text File	PDF
The Industrial Revolution	industrial.doc	industrial.pdf
Men of the Industrial Revolution	menrevolution.doc	menrevolution.pdf
European Immigration	european.doc	european.pdf
Asian Immigration	asian.doc	asian.pdf
World War I: The "Great War"	greatwar.doc	greatwar.pdf
The Roaring Twenties	twenties.doc	twenties.pdf
The Great Depression	depression.doc	depression.pdf
World War II in Europe	europe.doc	europe.pdf
World War II in the Pacific	pacific.doc	pacific.pdf
World War II Leaders	ww2leaders.doc	ww2leaders.pdf
The Civil Rights Movement	civilrights.doc	civilrights.pdf
Dr. Martin Luther King Jr.	king.doc	king.pdf
The Cold War	coldwar.doc	coldwar.pdf
Conflicts in the Middle East	middleeast.doc	middleeast.pdf
Modern World Leaders	worldleadrs.doc	worldleadrs.pdf

JPEG Files

The images found throughout the book are also provided on the Teacher Resource CD. See pages 141–143 for image descriptions, credits, and filenames.

Word Documents of Texts
- Change leveling further for individual students.
- Separate text and images for students who need additional help decoding the text.
- Resize the text for visually impaired students.

Teacher Resource CD

Full-Color PDFs of Texts
- Create overheads.
- Project texts for whole-class review.
- Read texts online.
- Email texts to parents or students at home.

JPEGs of Primary Sources
- Recreate cards at more levels for individual students.
- Use primary sources to spark interest or assess comprehension.

© *Shell Education*